Please Don't HURT ME

Leonard Keene

Revised by

Davis Keene

LUCIDBOOKS

Please Don't Hurt Me

Revised by Davis Keene

Published by Lucid Books in Houston, TX
www.LucidBooks.com

ISBN: 978-1-63296-981-1 (Paperback)
ISBN: 978-1-63296-982-8 (Hardback)
ISBN: 978-1-63296-990-3 (ebook)

Special Sales: Most Lucid Books titles are available in special quantity discounts. Custom imprinting or excerpting can also be done to fit special needs. Contact Lucid Books at Info@LucidBooks.com

For my grandfather, whose life and teaching pointed us to truth, and my grandmother, whose faith and strength preserved his legacy.

Contents

Author's Note

I never had the chance to meet my grandfather, but I've spent my life feeling the weight of his legacy. His principles, his conviction, and his commitment to God's Word have shaped the foundation of our family. The man I never met still speaks—through my father, through my grandmother, and through the values that have guided us since he went to be with the Lord too soon.

For those who have read his works, you'll recognize the heart behind these pages: a call to live with balance, integrity, and surrender to God's design. For those discovering his message for the first time, you'll find that it's just as relevant today as when he first wrote these words over fifty years ago. *Please Don't Hurt Me* is more than just a book to me and my family. It's a mirror that reflects timeless biblical truth, spoken with the clarity and passion of a man who lived what he taught.

This new edition exists to reignite that message for a new generation. While the principles remain the same, our world has changed, and so have the pressures that families face. My prayer is that this refreshed version will help you bridge the gap between the wisdom of yesterday and the challenges of today.

The ministry my grandfather began, Balanced Life Association, was built on the conviction that faith should touch every part of life. That same conviction continues today through the Legacy Alive Foundation that stands as both an heir and an extension of his vision. His original framework laid the foundation upon which Legacy Alive is being built: helping families live with faith at the center, balance as discipline, and generosity as lifestyle.

If you hold this book in your hands today, you're part of that story. You are the continuation of a legacy built on obedience, balance, and faithfulness. May these words challenge you, comfort you, and compel you to live with the same courage and conviction my grandfather modeled so well.

To My Grandfather:

Although we never met, I feel the ripple of your obedience in every part of my life. Your words shaped our family, your faith changed our story, and your example continues to inspire mine. I pray that as I carry your mission forward, I do so with the same humility and boldness that you lived with. I pray that I honor the truth you built your life on while breathing new life into the ministry you began.

With gratitude and reverence,
Davis Keene
Your Grandson

Introduction

Why are people so unhappy? Recently I traveled with my wife, Cloetta, and our two children, Randy and Joetta, on a holiday throughout the Eastern United States. As our Volkswagen bus chugged through the large cities with familiar names—New York; Washington, DC; Boston; and many others—we began to notice the faces of the people lost in large crowds, all in a hurry to go somewhere. But where? Why the hurry? How could they get so lost in such a large crowd? Are they really as lonely and hurt as they look? Look at each face. Some are tense and drawn. Some are blank with no emotion. Some have their faces twisted with an expression of pain as a prizefighter in a boxing match awaiting another hit in the face.

Randy said, "Dad, why are there so many unhappy people? They look like they have been hurt. Is there something we can do for them?"

Jesus looked on the masses and saw the hurts. He had compassion for them, for they were as sheep without a shepherd, with no one to care for their hurts. What is this book about? It's about healing the hurts of the people, having compassion for them, and doing something about it. Randy and I decided to name these hurt people. We called them "Wounded Walkers"—people who are up and around, walking, talking, working, and playing, but are wounded. Wounded deeply. They are Wounded Walkers.

Proverbs 18:14 (KJV) says, "The Spirit of a man will sustain his infirmity, but a wounded spirit who can bear?" The Wounded Walkers have wounds in their spirit. The pain is unbearable to many, so unbearable that suicide is now a national disease. Even professional counselors such as psychiatrists agree that suicide is a problem. The inability to heal these wounds frustrates many a counselor. This book has been written to illustrate how God can heal those wounded spirits.

The intercom buzzed with a loud sense of urgency. "Mr. Keene, your two o'clock appointment is here," the receptionist declared as she moved her mouth closer to the large receiver to speak. "Shall I show her in?" Before responding to the voice, I thought to myself, *Is there no end to the problems? I wonder what this lady's difficulty will be.*

Counseling is a painful process. In counseling, the root of the problem must be unearthed—dug up. Exposing root problems in a person's life is painful. It must be done carefully in order to not cause a deeper hurt. I suppose it is painful because it is much like pulling the roots of a plant out of the ground. The unearthing of roots tears loose some dirt. Perhaps that is why so many of us make such diligent effort to keep the root of our problems hidden from others' views. It's painful to change existing habits and behavioral patterns.

Some roots must be disturbed, while others must be torn out. Paul, the writer of Colossians, speaks of putting off the "old man" and putting on the "new man." It is painful but necessary. Happiness and peace of mind are at stake. Well, let's find out what this lady's trouble is.

"Cloetta, send her in." As the door opened, I looked up to see the new client. She was blonde and attractive. She was tall, perhaps 5'8", slim, and well-dressed. She moved toward my desk with a sense of sureness. She knew her purpose and her destination. I arose.

The receptionist spoke. "Mr. Keene, I would like you to meet Sandra Lee. She has an appointment with you for two o'clock." Sandra reached out to shake my hand. I responded by taking a firm hold. Her hand was warm and wet. Hands often tell inner feelings. Through the nervousness of her handshake, I could detect that Sandra probably had much inner frustration. She was covering her inner frustrations well, except for her hands. Her hands gave her away. I suppose this is true of most people. Their hands tell on them—bitten off nails, nervousness, sweating, busy, calm, or well-groomed. All these tend to identify the person within.

"Sandra, I'm glad to know you. Will you be seated, please?" indicating the chair in front of the desk. "Cloetta, will you please stay? You can sit over here to my left," I added.

Sandra glanced toward me with a look of bewilderment and asked, "Mr. Keene, why is the receptionist staying?"

My response was to the point. "Her presence will prevent a number of traps from hindering our counseling session. Many people have been injured by failure to listen to the warnings of the danger that exists between a male counselor and a female client. The receptionist's presence will help keep us on the correct path. The only alternative would be to have an aged lady counsel you. Paul once told Titus something like this: 'You can counsel the aged men, you can counsel the young men, you can counsel the aged women, but you leave the young women alone.' That's my translation of Titus 2:1–6. It is either this way, or we'll have an aged woman counsel you."

"I understand," was Sandra's quick reply.

Chapter 1

Counseling Women

"Have you discussed this problem with your husband?" Many women who come for counseling have not discussed their problem with their husband. The reasons vary from "he won't listen" to "he wouldn't understand" to "I'm afraid of him." Many divorce summonses served upon the husband by the sheriff or process server are a surprise to the husband. This should not be. One of the primary goals of the counselor should be to prepare the wife to discuss the problem openly and in a spirit of love with her husband.

She should be instructed not to say, "Mr. Keene says this and that." This type of comment brought home to the husband by the wife after a counseling session will only add gasoline to an existing fire. It is rejection by implication. I reject you; I accept my counselor as my model. She is saying, "I approve of Mr. Keene (the counselor), and I want you to be like him." The husband often interprets these comments as rejection by the wife. He is hurt. He then will either turn away—spending his spare time on airplanes, boats, motorcycles, extra work, or other women—or he will explode, lashing out at the unseen counselor who is stealing the admiration of his wife.

I leaned back in my chair and said, "Tell me about your problem, Sandra."

"Well, it is not really my problem. It is my husband. He is really the problem."

"In what way is your husband the problem?" I asked.

"He shuts me out of his life. He works hard. When he comes home, he turns on the television and begins to watch the news. He won't talk to me. When I speak to him or try to tell him my feelings, he won't listen. Mr. Keene, he just won't listen to me. I've tried to talk to him at bedtime, but he says, 'Save it until morning, Sandra.' In the morning, he is too busy to listen." She ended with a deep sigh.

"Has this always been the case between you and him?" I asked.

"Yes," she replied as she settled back into her chair.

"I noticed from the information sheet that your husband, Richard, is twenty-seven years old, and you are twenty-three. You have been married for two years. What was it like the first year of your marriage?" I slid the information sheet forward so it was more visible for her reference.

The Information Sheet

An information sheet should be filled out before you talk with the client concerning their problem. The information sheet should be designed so it prepares you with much-needed information and will also prepare the client for the painful process of exposing personal information to a stranger.

As Sandra glanced toward the information sheet she had filled out previously, she began to tell me about her husband, Richard. "We have always had difficulty communicating. Even from the start. He just will not let me get close to him. Do you know what I mean? If I get too close to the 'real Richard,' he shuts me off. When he shuts me off, I feel hurt and rejected. As you can see, Mr. Keene, from the information sheet, Richard travels some and is away from home several days a month. I used to look forward to his coming home. I would be excited about his arrival. I'd also be sad when he left on his business trips. But recently it is almost the reverse. I'm often glad he is gone. It is a relief to see him walk out the door to begin one of his three- or four-day business trips. Actually, I don't think I love him anymore. I haven't told Richard, but I've even begun thinking about a divorce. I know divorce is wrong, but I don't know what else to do."

Imbalance

Everything about God's creation is designed for balance. It seems that most animals, trees, and insects are preprogrammed to maintain this balance. It is only man who has been given such choice that he can violate God's system of balance at will. I can remember as a boy, maybe ten years old, watching a squirrel carry acorns by the dozens to his hole in the tree. He was programmed to store food for one winter. The little squirrel was completely engrossed in his preparation for hard times when the snow fell. He was also programmed to know just how many acorns would get him through the winter. No more, No less.

But on the other hand, it is man who, with a free will and a choice, decides to begin storing "acorns" (money, property, and influence) for two years, five years, twenty years, and the next generation ahead. Once man gets his "extra acorns" deposited in the tree, he becomes fear-oriented—fearful that others will come and steal his advanced supply. He becomes unbalanced by his over-concern for "acorn security" in the future. I have found many of the problems facing the counselor is an unbalanced person sitting across the desk.

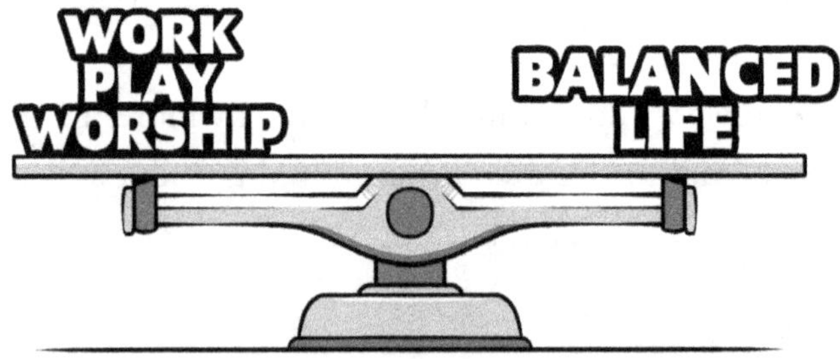

He tends to overdo one of the above or leave one or more completely out of his life. A person who works without play and worship is headed for problems. He is out of balance. Many people work and play but fail to worship. That inner desire to worship is never met.

"Sandra," I replied, "did you love Richard when you married him two years ago?"

"Oh, yes," she answered.

"Sandra, before we go further in this counseling session, I want to show you something concerning successful counseling. You need to understand the things I'm about to show you before we can solve your problem. Counseling is not a panacea. Counseling is not a cure-all. It is only a method of locating, cleaning, applying medication, and dressing the wound, so to speak. I call it a Band-Aid program. I can only *lead you* to solve your own problem. I can show you how to obtain the surgery that is necessary to *root out* a difficulty. But I can't do it for you. Do you understand what I'm saying?"

Sandra leaned forward on the arms of her chair with interest and replied, "Yes, Mr. Keene, I believe I do understand. You are saying that it is sort of like leading a horse to water. He has to be the one that drinks for himself."

"Right! Counseling is a delicate balance between the client discovering the problem and the counselor revealing the truth as he sees it. I call this delicate balance the Show and Tell scales. Let me draw a picture of the scales on this chalkboard."

As I moved toward the chalkboard on the easel by my desk, I added, "I like to draw diagrams and pictures. We tend to think in pictures. The difficulty with most counseling is that the client spends most of her time on the Show side of the balance. The counselor insists the client discover all her own problems by a series of counseling sessions. Then the client ventilates by telling all her innermost problems. As she hears herself talk out what is on the inside, she begins to discover her problem. As she discovers her problem through her own speaking, the counselor should begin guiding by telling the truth regarding correct human behavior. The client shows by talking, and then a process of discovery takes place within her. At the same time, the counselor from time to time *Tells* by revealing the truth in love. Do you see this balance, Sandra?"

Show and Tell

The classical method of counseling is too heavy on the *Show* side of the scales. The counselor lets the client talk—hours, days, weeks, months, years—until she vents and *Shows* all that is within her. But there's not much *Tell* by the counselor. "Should I stop sleeping with different men?" "Well it depends. Tell me more." Too much *Show*. Not enough *Tell*. They have so little truth to tell that they simply keep quiet and listen. A religious counselor tends to be heavy on the *Tell*. The client *Shows* for ten minutes, and the counselor bursts forth with a thirty-minute *Tell* of shoulds and ought-tos. He too is out of balance on the *Tell*. The client is not given sufficient time to *Show*.

"As you begin to talk and disclose personal things about your life, Sandra, you will find yourself tending to discover problem areas. I will from time to time reveal the truth to you regarding your problem. We will attempt together to strike a correct level on the *Show and Tell* balance. Do you agree with the use of this principle in our counseling session today?"

Sandra smiled at Cloetta, looked back at me, and said, "Yes, sir. I do agree."

Chapter 2

Build the Relationship

Many people who come for help have been hurt and betrayed by intimate associates. Perhaps a husband or a wife has been disloyal. A best friend, employer, relative, pastor, parent or a child—someone has hurt the client. In the first and second hour of the session, carefully allow a relationship to develop that sounds of loyalty and trustworthiness. 1 Thessalonians 2:11–12 tells us how: "For you know how, like a father with his children, we *exhorted* each one of you and *encouraged* you and *charged* you to walk in a manner worthy of God" (emphasis added).

To *exhort* means to teach and show the truth. If the clients knew the truth, they would not likely be seeking your help. It may be that they know right from wrong, but they may not know how acting on that knowledge will become truth and set them free. It is up to you to guide truth into their lives as a father does with his children. To *encourage* in this context means to show in your attitude, action, and words that "I care about you, and I'm here to suffer with you and help you reduce that suffering."

The greater the crowd, the more people will be suffering. Jesus discerned this as he ministered to the thousands. The Bible says he was moved with compassion, for they had no shepherd. A shepherd examines his sheep for wounds and hurts. He then ministers to those sheep that are suffering. At least for a short time the counselor becomes the shepherd to the "wounded sheep" he is counseling. Don't be a head-nodder. Some people in counseling get you to agree with a few fundamentals. As you agree and nod your head, you'll nod in agreement when they try to convince you that their behavior is right and everyone else is wrong. Don't be a head-nodder.

To *charge* means to let the client know he must act. He must do something to help recover himself out of his suffering. 2 Timothy 2:24–26 says:

> *And the Lord's servant [the counselor] must not be quarrelsome but kind to everyone [the client], able to teach, patiently enduring evil, correcting his opponents [the client] with gentleness. God may perhaps grant them repentance leading to a knowledge of the truth, and they [the client] may come to their senses and escape from the snare [place of hurt] of the devil, after being captured by him to do his will.*

Let the client discover that you have no secret formula or immediate cure-all for his problem, but you are willing to teach, love, and help him recover from his place of suffering. A relationship between client and counselor builds. No betrayals.

Step number one in counseling: Build the relationship by *exhorting*, by *encouraging*, and by *charging* as a father does his children.

"Tell me, Sandra, has your husband ever had a close relationship with anyone in his life?"

Sandra thought for a minute and then answered. "No, I imagine our relationship is his closest one."

"What about his parents? Tell me about his father and mother."

"Well, Richard's father was an alcoholic. I don't know too much about him except that he gave his family a pretty bad time. He is supposed to be somewhere in Oregon. Actually, I have never met him. I don't even know what he looks like. Richard doesn't like to talk about his dad. He says he doesn't hate him; he just doesn't like him, just as he doesn't like cottage cheese. However, Richard's mother is a sweetheart. She worked and raised Richard, his brother, and sister. Richard does have a pretty close relationship with his mother and his brother."

"Sandra, is there anyone else your husband dislikes?"

"I don't think so," she replied. "He is really a pretty friendly guy. He is one of his company's top salesmen. Oh, wait. There is one old buddy who betrayed Richard by lying to other friends. That was way back in high school though. I suppose Richard dislikes that old buddy. Mr. Keene, what are you probing for? What are you trying to get to? Is there something here that I'm missing?" Sandra asked nervously.

"Yes, Sandra, there is, and I can illustrate by showing you a *broken relationship* and its consequence. Suppose Mr. A and Mr. B are communicating, and because of that interaction, Mr. A gets hurt and begins to dislike Mr. B. Let's draw another diagram." Reaching the chalkboard, I erased the last diagram.

Sandra spoke quietly. "Mr. Keene, could I have some paper so I can take notes and also draw some of the diagrams?" Cloetta opened a drawer near her and handed a small stack of paper and a pen to Sandra.

"The hurt that was created by the interaction caused a dislike or hatred in Mr. A," I began. "That breaks the relationship between A and B. Mr. A has a broken relationship with Mr. B. They may still work together and they may still see one another, but nonetheless, there is a broken relationship. We can identify this broken relationship by inserting a bolt of bitterness across the communication flow between Mr. A and Mr. B."

"But, Mr. Keene, what is so strange about a broken relationship? There are many broken relationships. Doesn't everybody have broken relationships?" Sandra appeared puzzled.

"Many people do, Sandra. But watch the next step. Mr. A now leaves the presence of Mr. B and goes to meet Mr. X. Mr. A cannot completely keep his attention on Mr. X because his mind and emotions are still fixed on Mr. B and the broken relationship. Mr. A cannot successfully relate to Mr. X because of the past broken relationship. That broken relationship hinders his ability to deal successfully with Mr. X."

Sandra arose and walked toward the chalkboard as she spoke. "I still don't quite understand how a broken relationship can affect a person's ability to deal with other people."

"Sandra, do you believe in God?" I asked.

"Yes," she replied as she sat down in her chair.

"Sandra, have you accepted Jesus as your Savior?"

"Yes," she replied again with a more determined ring in her voice.

"Now, one more question. Do you believe in the Bible?"

"Oh yes. How could anyone not believe in the Bible?" she declared.

"1 John 2:9–11 holds the secret to understanding broken relationships and how they work. Here, let me read it to you." Reaching toward the corner of my desk, I picked up my Bible. The old Bible was beginning to become frayed around the edges. I thought of using the new one in that same drawer but really didn't want to retire this old treasure. Turning to 1 John, I began to read.

> *Whoever says he is in the light and hates his brother is still in darkness. Whoever loves his brother abides in the light, and in him there is no cause for stumbling. But whoever hates his brother is in the darkness and walks in the darkness, and does not know where he is going, because the darkness has blinded his eyes.*

"Notice the verse says whoever hates his brother is in darkness. In other translations, it says he is *blinded.* We can call this blindness a *blind spot*—something you can't see. A good illustration would be like driving a car. Suppose I am in the right-hand lane and decide to move into the left-hand lane. I look in the mirror to check the traffic to my side. I see nothing. It all appears clear. It looks safe for me to change lanes, so I start making my lane change. 'Beep-beep' a horn to my left blares out. I swerve back to my lane. How did that car get beside me? I looked but didn't see him. He was in my blind spot. The danger was there all the time; I just did not see it."

Mr. Keene drew a diagram and sat back down. "This is much the same with broken relationships. The danger is there, but we are blinded by the broken relationship. We have a blind spot. One more illustration. When I was in the Army, I was on the boxing team. I soon learned how to win some of the prize fights—simply do something during the boxing match that will frustrate my opponent. He will soon become irritated and very angry with me. As he becomes angry, he will begin losing his ability to make wise decisions in the boxing match. He soon begins to swing wildly. He has blind spots from his hatred and dislike for me. All I had to do to defeat this opponent was wait for his wild punch. As he swings wildly, I move in with a well-placed blow to his head. He is now on his way to defeat—defeated because of the blind spot caused by his broken relationship with me. Broken relationships cause blind spots that stop us from acting wisely."

Chapter 3

The Five Basic Relationships

Most people have at least five basic relationships. Each relationship is different and requires separate attention.

1. God → Self
2. Self → Self
3. Husband → Wife
4. Parent → Child
5. Self → Others

A broken relationship on any level will show up in the other levels. For example, if a man has a broken relationship at work with a boss or coworker, that will show up in the way he treats his wife and family. He may not realize he has changed, but his wife and children can tell you. Life is not as enjoyable for them. If this man does not act promptly to heal the original broken relationship at work, it will cause other relationships to break. Perhaps he abuses his wife, and that fosters further hurt. Most certainly the broken relationship is going to affect his ability to communicate with God. We have a simple policy about this at our house: Don't break a relationship. It's not worth the price you pay. Remember, a broken relationship in one area will affect all other areas of relationships. Guard against the "*Bolt of Bitterness.*"

Definition of Broken Relationships

When two or more people interact, it is possible for hate, fear, resentment, jealousy, bitterness, unforgiveness, or anger to rise up within the heart of one or more of the people involved.

Sandra's face flushed red as excitement arose within her. "Boy! Do you mean to tell me the reason Richard is not able to treat me correctly is because of the broken relationship he has with his father? Do I understand correctly what you are saying about the effects of broken relationships, Mr. Keene? Richard does not realize he is treating me badly? Is that a correct observation?"

I leaned back in my chair with a warm sense of satisfaction sweeping through my spirit and responded, "You are learning fast."

Sandra continued. "But how do we get Richard to fix these broken relationships with his father and former friend if he does not realize how it's hurting both himself and me?"

"Sandra, we will handle that question later. First, we need to apply this to you!"

"What do you mean, apply this to me?" she asked.

"You do recall telling me a few moments ago that you felt you no longer love Richard, right?" Sandra responded by a nod of her head. "Let me ask you this? What would be the most harmful thing you could do to Richard if you wanted to hurt him?"

"Stop loving him, I suppose," she said rather quietly. "Take away my love from him."

"Often, Sandra, when we are hurt and injured by other people, it is natural to react by stopping our flow of love to that person. It often becomes an automatic reaction to injury. If someone hurts me, I will automatically stop my flow of love toward that person. They no longer deserve my love. Therefore, we stop the flow of love."

"Mr. Keene, do you think my feelings of no love for Richard were a reaction to his injury to me? That I am just returning hurt for hurt?" she replied with a near frightened look on her face.

"It is an easy trap to fall into, Sandra."

Sandra started to speak again. "Why couldn't I see it before I came for counseling? Do I have blind spots? Oh, my goodness. If I have blind spots, that means I have broken relationships."

I walked to the door and opened it. Looking back at Cloetta I asked, "Could you bring us three cups of coffee? I think we are going to need it."

Cloetta asked before leaving the room, "Do you use cream or sugar, Sandra?"

Sandra shook her head no and then went on talking. "I don't think I have a broken relationship with anyone. Well, maybe. I used to date a guy. His name was Buddy, but that was three or four years ago. It still wouldn't bother me now—would it?"

I returned to my chair and began to answer her question. "Broken relationships get worse as the years pass. I've known people who still had the effects of broken relationships forty-two years later, still harboring the bitterness and resentment of the broken relationship. Broken relationships usually are what make the retirement years (the so-called Golden Years) so unpleasant for many people. Time does not heal broken relationships. Let me repeat, time does not heal broken relationships.

Roots of Bitterness

Roots of bitterness are the result of hurts and wrongs done to us by others. If a person responds incorrectly to a hurt or wrongdoing, a root of bitterness is established within his or her heart. This bitterness will spring up, troubling both the person harboring the bitterness and also defiling many others. Put another way, bitterness within a person is a polluting agent that defiles people in the immediate environment. Watch how easy it is to fall into line and agree when a man at a social gathering begins to criticize and speak hate toward a person who isn't there. It's so simple to agree with that criticism and begin to develop a similar root of bitterness in yourself. You become convinced that the absent person has wronged you also.

Hebrews 12:14–15 says, "Strive for peace with everyone, and for the holiness without which no one will see the Lord. See to it that no one fails to obtain the grace of God; that no 'root of bitterness' springs up and causes trouble, and by it many become defiled." A husband and wife can "taste the bitterness" in each other's attitude, speech, and conduct. It pollutes the environment (the home and children). Balanced Life Counseling is aimed at eradicating this bitterness so people can truly open up to one another, submit to one another, and love one another in a meaningful way.

"Sandra, I'll be showing you the proper therapy for healing broken relationships a little later in this counseling session. But we still need to discover more of the root problem and learn more truth." Picking up my Bible I turned back to Hebrews 12:14–15 about striving for peace and not letting a "root of bitterness" spring up. "Roots of bitterness from broken relationships spring up quickly, without warning, causing trouble in you and defiling many others." The door opened behind Sandra, and Cloetta came in quietly. She set a cup of steaming coffee in front of Sandra and handed me another. She quickly slipped back into her chair.

Sandra asked, "Mr. Keene, may I tell you something very personal?"

"Yes, Sandra, you may," I answered.

"Well, when Richard rejects me—." Sandra paused as if trying to make certain what came out was right. "Like when I need to talk to him so desperately I think my insides are going to come apart. I try to pull him from his television, and he either ignores me or pretends to listen but doesn't." Sandra paused, fighting back the tears. "He just tells me to leave him alone. I feel so rejected. I feel so all alone. And do you know what flashes into my mind? A gray image of Buddy. You know, the old boyfriend. Sometimes he is sneering at me. Sometimes he is trying to hurt me. Sometimes he is just standing there with a blank stare. I get a sick feeling down in the pit of my stomach. I wonder if this image flash of Buddy is a root of bitterness. Do you think it is a root of bitterness that is described in the verses you just read? Do I really have resentment, unforgiveness, and bitterness toward Buddy? Boy, the more I talk, the more I believe I do have a broken relationship with him. I tried to forgive him for the wrongs he did to me. I thought I had forgiven him. But I can see now that there is still unforgiveness down in my spirit. I am still hurt by the way he treated me. He hurt me, and I still haven't gotten over it."

"Yes, Sandra, and when Richard rejects you, he hurts you. That old root of bitterness springs up, troubling you and affecting others. Unforgiveness can only be eradicated by an act of your will to forgive—plus a *spiritual happening* on the inside. Simply an act of willing forgiveness is not always enough. You need help to pull up the roots of bitterness caused by the broken relationship."

Before I could go on, Sandra broke in. "Mr. Keene, I want to get this thing out of my system. I don't want to live this way any longer. Life is not getting better. Life is getting worse. I need to find the answer. I am too young, and I want a happy life, not one filled with bitterness."

Need of Counsel

"Without counsel plans fail, but with many advisers they [the plans] succeed" (Prov. 15:22). There are a lot of Lone Ranger Christians running around today doing their own thing—accountable to no one. "It's just me and Jesus" they burst forth with a spirit of rebellion in their attitude. "I won't have anyone tell me what to do." Be careful, Mr. Lone Ranger Christian. As one brother said, "God may take your gun, shoot your horse, and send your saddle home."

God is saying to Christians everywhere to open up and submit yourselves to one another. You need the strength and security of a multitude of counselors. Get yourself a shepherd. Become a shepherd. Get into a sheepfold before the storm comes. We need one another to assist in working out our imperfections and hang-ups. God is beckoning on the one hand with commitment, loyalty, and obedience. Satan is beckoning on the other hand with rebellion, oppression, promise-breaking, and doing your own thing. God's road leads to success and peace; Satan's road leads to failure and conflict.

"Sandra, have you heard the story of John the Baptist and how he was beheaded by King Herod at the request of a dancing girl and her mother? The story is found in the Bible in Matthew Chapter 14. At that time, John and Jesus were best friends. John was the one who had baptized Jesus. John was in a special relationship with our Lord. What do you suppose Jesus felt when he learned of the death of his best friend, particularly when he discovered the uselessness of John's death? John was killed because of the plotting evilness of a mother and daughter who tricked the king into making an oath to give the daughter her request. What was her request? John's head on a serving tray! When Jesus learned of this, he departed into a desert, and the people followed him. It would have been easy for Jesus to have allowed unforgiveness to rise up at that time. It would have been easy to tell the people to go away so he could be alone in his grief over the death of his best friend. But Jesus did not respond to the hurt that way. Instead, Matthew 14:14 says, 'When he went ashore he saw a great crowd, and he had compassion on them and healed their sick.' What followed were three miracles in the ministry of Jesus. He healed the sick, he multiplied the fish and bread to feed thousands, and he walked on water. Three of the great miracles Jesus performed were right after he *responded correctly* to the hurt done to him by the death of John. Now, Sandra, notice carefully the sequence of events. Number One: The wrong done to Jesus (murder of his friend). Number Two: A correct response to the wrong. Number Three: The miracles followed."

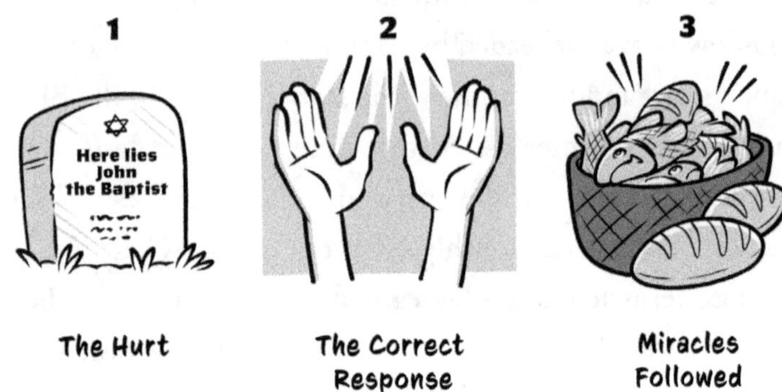

I stopped to go to the chalkboard and draw an illustration. "Notice again, Sandra. The wrong done, the correct response to the wrong, and then miracles followed. And we wonder why we as Christians are so helpless. We have not responded correctly to wrongs and hurts. If we would learn to respond correctly, the miracles would follow."

"I see it! I see it! I see!" Sandra blurted out. She reached over and took Cloetta's hand as she sat in silence for the next few moments. The awareness of this truth was sinking deep into her spirit. An expression of joy began to shine from her face. We all sat there silently for a few moments. I did not want to spoil the moment of truth for Sandra by more conversation. As we sat silently, I thought to myself, *The next step in this counseling session must be delicately led by the Holy Spirit.*

A key principle in counseling is hidden in Proverbs 14:10: "The heart knows its own bitterness, and no stranger shares its joy." People get a certain joy from their own bitterness (unforgiveness toward others). It's the "I hate her and I won't stop hating her because it feels good to me" syndrome. I have found many clients who would not give up their resentment and bitterness toward a father, mother, church member, or former business partner because there was joy in maintaining that bitterness. I can remember the thirty-five-year-old preacher who was so hurt by another pastor that he began plotting ways to get even, plotting ways to get revenge. He later told me that he actually enjoyed mentally visualizing how he would hurt him back.

He saw how he would take a gun and shoot him in the head. Or it's like the husband or wife who nourishes and cherishes their bitterness caused by the other in the past—continually bringing up old faults because there is joy in remembrance. A counselor must recognize that people get joy from their own bitterness. We must also recognize that no stranger shares in its joy. We are strangers to the heart of the client.

It is natural for the heart of the client filled with bitterness to exclude all others from looking in—to exclude all strangers from sharing in it. Why? Simply because of the shame attached to exposure—exposure of the insides of that person. Often, if clients in frustration and panic are encouraged to let the counselor look too quickly on the inside, hatred for the counselor will be the result. The counselor is a stranger sharing in the joy of the heart's bitterness. The client may turn his bitterness toward the counselor. Instead of eradicating the bitterness, there is now even more bitterness.

Chapter 4

The Suffering Heroine

Jamie, age twenty-seven, was divorced three years ago. It was a stormy marriage and a bitter separation. The court case with lawyers, counselors, judges, and relatives' interference was a nightmare. Now it's all over. Jamie says to herself, "Never again will I allow myself to be exposed to such hurt and misery. From now on it's just Todd and me." Todd is Jamie's son, age four. Jamie reasons to herself, "I will not allow Todd to be hurt like I was hurt. Life will be better for him. I'll make sure of it."

Jamie begins to take on an attitude determined to insulate Todd from injury of the world—at her own expense. In fact, she says, "I don't care what it costs me or how much I give up. Todd is going to have a good life." Jamie is becoming a suffering heroine. She is a heroine (in her own eyes) by laying her life down for her son. She is suffering and will soon let all the audience watching her know that she is suffering. She plays the role with gallant and might—the "think-only-of-Todd" mother.

What's the promise? Life will get more unpleasant for Jamie. Her attitude and role-playing as a suffering heroine will deter the development of any genuine relationship. She will become more lonely, more bitter. When Todd reaches adulthood, Jamie may develop illnesses that will assist in holding Todd to an unspoken commitment. You see, Todd owes his mother a great deal for her having sacrificed her life and happiness for his welfare. Todd may feel guilty about establishing his own life. There are many "Jamies" and many "Todds" at various stages of this game called becoming a suffering heroine. What is Jamie saying by her conduct? "I want two things from you. I want you to feel sorry for me, and I want you to stay away from me. You might hurt me." It requires a great deal of patience in counseling the Jamies and Todds. They both must be schooled and motivated to develop other close relationships. The old hurt from the previous relationship hinders building new ones. With this in mind, it is often necessary to follow the steps to remove the hurt, as will be demonstrated in Sandra's case.

The heart knows its own bitterness. It knows where the problem is rooted. It then becomes necessary to let a person "discover it" and in general terms confess the fault of bitterness to the counselor. I have found that it is not necessary to have the client tell me all the details. In Sandra's case, the fact that her old boyfriend, Buddy, had wronged her was sufficient confession on her part to begin the spiritual healing that was necessary. A counselor often falls into the trap of listening to and encouraging discussion of intricate details of the wrongdoing of the client, or details of the wrong done to the client. There is a large segment of the counseling world that practices such full and deep disclosure. I recommend against it for several reasons.

1. Reliving the sexual assaults, the promiscuity, and any other wrongful conduct in detail often creates new injuries, wounds, and guilt.
2. Intimate details activate the perverse nature of man—his body lust, his lust of the eye—and greed on the part of the counselor.
3. Counselor and client reliving every detail is much like seeing an X-rated movie.
4. Ephesians 5:11–14 says, "Take no part in the unfruitful works of darkness, but instead expose them. For it is shameful even to speak of the things that they do in secret. But when anything is exposed by the light, it becomes visible, for anything that becomes visible is light."

Such detail becomes permanently imprinted on the mind of all persons present. What counselor can sit six to ten hours a day watching X-rated movies and still maintain his sanity? How can he expect to walk in the spirit and not lust after the things of the flesh? I suspect the very fact so many counselors listen to and encourage the discussion of gory details is why psychiatrists have a large percentage of suicide. The human mind and spirit cannot bear the continual supply of perverse thoughts. For this same reason, many active pastors in churches get sidetracked. They focus on the things of the flesh rather than the things of the Spirit.

Sandra had begun to relax and enter a new state of peace. “Are you ready to begin the steps to get the hurt out?” I stood to prepare myself to write again on the chalkboard.

“Yes, Mr. Keene, I am ready.” Sandra looked up smiling and released Cloetta’s hand. Cloetta smiled and slid a few more sheets of paper to Sandra to be sure she had an ample supply.

“Alright, here goes,” and I began writing.

Step Number 1: See yourself through the eyes of the wrongdoer.

"Examine your own response to the wrongdoer's behavior. What problem did Buddy have that affected the way he treated you? Did Buddy have broken relationships? If he did, he may not have realized he was treating you incorrectly. He may have been blinded by broken relationships with his father, mother, or some other person. Remember, Sandra, blind spots often cause bad behavior. This bad behavior is easily interpreted by others as selfishness. He may not realize he was acting selfishly. He may have been blinded to the real significance of his acts and how they hurt you."

"Wow! I never thought of it that way. You mean to tell me that he may not have realized he was hurting me?" Sandra asked.

"That's correct. He still may not realize he wronged you," I replied. "Let's go on to the second step."

Step Number 2: Reexamine your response.

"It is not what happens to us that counts," I said. "It's how we respond. Each of us is going to have hundreds and thousands of people wrong or hurt us throughout our lifetime. Even a life of isolation (the little old hermit in a cabin) will still have people interfering and hurting him. 'It's my privacy. It's my rights. Who do they think they are? How dare they take advantage of me like that. It's not fair. Get off my property.' There is a constant supply of people hurting him and injuring his rights. Wherever I go, people will be abusing me—waitresses spilling coffee, cooks who are slow, traffic jams, people late for a meeting, people trying to get my money, people who are unappreciative, people who take advantage, people who curse me, people who are stingy and out-fumble me at lunch so I end up paying the $60 bill, courts that do not appear to do justice, police who won't respond to calls, neighbors who won't keep their dogs quiet, a mother or father who neglected me—and on and on. A book could be written listing the numerous wrongs people will force upon me over my lifetime. So the answer is not how to stop these people from wronging me. Let me repeat. The answer is not how to stop these people from wronging me. The answer is how to react correctly toward wrongful behavior. That is the secret to happiness and peace."

Chapter 5

Crisis, Danger, or Opportunity?

A crisis is a situation where things do not go our way. People are not doing what we expected. My wife forgot to pick up my good suit at the dry cleaners. Crisis! The car breaks down on the freeway, leaving me stranded. Crisis strikes again! The neighbor's dogs get in the flower beds. The cats fight at 2:00 a.m. Crisis! I lost a business deal costing thousands of dollars and many hours of time. Crisis strikes again! Life has one to as many as a hundred crises a day in store for each person. Avoiding crisis is not the problem. There will always be crisis as long as you can move and breathe. The real issue is how you *respond* to the crisis. If a person responds to crisis with impatience, anger, anxiety, or rudeness to others, he has picked up the *danger* part of crisis. The danger now destroys his happiness and his health, and injures people around who receive the burst of this anger, impatience, and anxiety.

Recently I noticed a man at the airport. It appeared that his luggage was delayed. He went into a frenzy, speaking out hate, anger, and curses. His luggage was lost. "Incompetent help! No one can do anything right anymore!" What a sight. The sixty-or-something-year-old acted like a six-year-old. "For this people's heart has grown dull, and with their ears they can barely hear, and their eyes they have closed" (Matt. 13:15). It was a grown man who simply did not know how to react correctly to a crisis. His heart had grown dull, and he did not see his own actions. The *opportunity* part of crisis is to allow yourself to grow in love, joy, peace, patience, kindness, goodness, faithfulness, gentleness, and self-control.

Begin to recognize the danger part of crisis. Make a conscientious effort to *only pick up the opportunity side of crisis.* Hebrews 12:1 says, "Therefore, since we are surrounded by so great a cloud of witnesses, let us also lay aside every weight, and sin which clings so closely, and let us run with endurance the race that is set before us."

"Do you see what I'm talking about, Sandra?" I asked.

"Can you explain a little more? It isn't quite clear to me," she responded, frankly.

"Well, Sandra, you being a Christian and having accepted the Lordship of Jesus in your life, you also recognize that Satan does exist, do you not?" I paused for her to respond.

"Oh, yes!" she replied. "God's Word declares that all power has been given to Jesus."

"So all real power is of the Lord. The only power Satan has is to deceive, lie, and suggest. Satan does have power of suggestion to other people, making them treat you badly. He can suggest to the other person that they should wrong you. Where is the battle then? It is in the mind. 2 Corinthians 10:3–5 says, 'For though we walk in the flesh, we are not waging war according to the flesh. For the weapons of our warfare are not of the flesh but have divine power to destroy strongholds. We destroy arguments and every lofty opinion raised against the knowledge of God, and take every thought captive to obey Christ.'"

I waited for Sandra to take that all in and then added, "*Arguments* and *lofty opinions* are two things we are to destroy. Lofty opinions refer to the proud and self-exalting ideas in our minds. These are the things that raise themselves against the knowledge of God. The mind, Sandra, is the battleground. It is our obligation to destroy these things. We have control of our thoughts. Jesus said in Matthew Chapter 6 not to be anxious about life, what we will eat or drink, or about our body. Jesus said to 'seek first the kingdom of God and his righteousness, and all these things [food, clothing, houses, cars, status, money, etc.] will be added to you.' The kingdom of God is defined in the Bible not as food or drink but as righteousness, peace, and joy in the Holy Spirit."

"Excuse me, Mr. Keene. Where is that found in the Bible?" asked Sandra.

"Romans 14:17," I told her.

Sandra had made a note of each scripture I referred to. "So, then," I said, "what are the weapons in the battle? What are the weapons of our warfare? The verse says they are not of the flesh but mighty *through divine power* to destroy strongholds." Moving my Bible aside, I located the chalk and rose once again to the chalkboard. "I'll diagram what these weapons are and what the use of these weapons accomplishes."

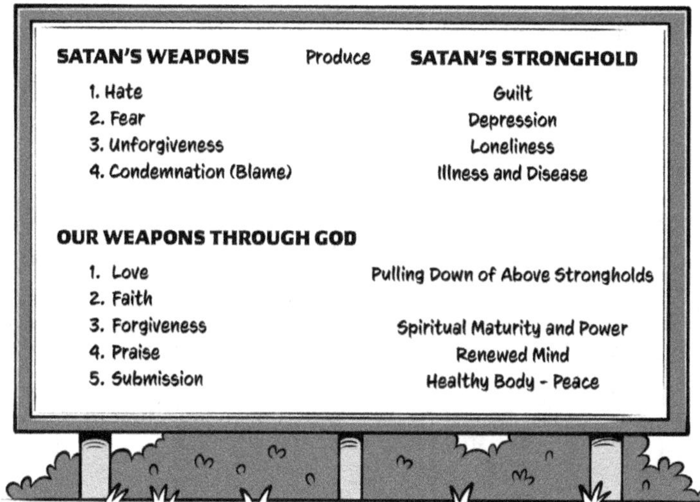

As I sat down, I said, "Sandra, I want to teach you something about counseling. Notice the weapons of the enemy—hate, fear, and unforgiveness. They are the very things that are involved in a broken relationship. If I am deceived into picking up one of these weapons to fight off a person who is hurting me, I have established a stronghold in my life—a stronghold of guilt, a stronghold of depression, a stronghold of loneliness, or a stronghold of illness and disease. Now we can see why Jesus did not use Satan's weapons when John the Baptist was beheaded. Instead, Jesus picked up one of our weapons (through God) and pulled down the stronghold, thereby renewing His mind and elevating His own spiritual maturity. Jesus learned to grow in stature physically and spiritually. We are to do the same. We are to learn to pick up the correct weapons to destroy the strongholds."

Some counselors erroneously instruct clients to pick up the weapon of condemnation and blame. But all that does is further establish the stronghold of guilt, depression, loneliness, illness, and disease in their client's life. They tell their clients that their faulty reaction to people is not their fault. They say their reaction was caused by a father who mistreated them when they were young. My problem, they may say, is caused by a mother who didn't spank me, a mother who abandoned me, or because I grew up in a depressed neighborhood. That's blaming and condemning someone else for my problem—transferring blame to others.

"Sandra, let's put a balance scale on the board to demonstrate how blame and condemnation *appear* to pull down a stronghold but actually do not." After erasing the chalkboard, I drew a balance scale and put guilt, depression, and loneliness on one side.

"The person is out of balance with so much guilt, depression, and loneliness. If the stronghold gets too heavy, the scale will eventually lower. When the scale tips, the person may have a mental relapse, a nervous breakdown, or a serious mental emotional disorder. They lose sight of reality. Life is no longer real. Reality is too painful so the person slips into a life of unreal problems—hallucinations, nightmares—and excessive fears now dominate the person's life. Thoughts are no longer controlled by the person but by Satan. Emotions are now out of control. The person may not be able to control his will. He may not be able to control his body."

I went back to my chair and sat down. "Blame and condemnation are used by some counselors to adjust this scale. They put blame and condemnation on the right-hand side of this scale. The weight of the blame and condemnation will lift the guilt, depression, and loneliness up so there is a balance."

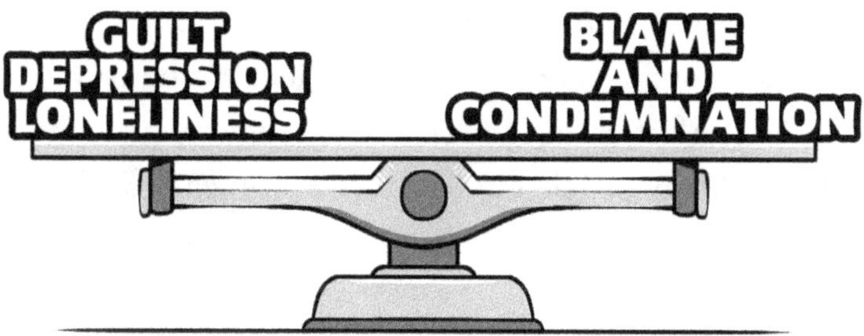

I pointed to the chalkboard. "For a while this appears to work. Blame mother, father, sister. Blame the boss, blame the ex-husband or ex-wife, blame someone, blame anyone—but don't blame me. There is no real success in using this type of counseling therapy. The client often ends up in worse condition. She has just used another of Satan's weapons (condemnation and blame), and it will not pull down the stronghold. It only adds to it. Romans 2:1 says, 'Therefore you have no excuse, O man, every one of you who judges. For in passing judgment on another you condemn yourself, because you, the judge, practice the very same things.'"

I went on to explain condemnation and blame. "Condemnation and blame are evidence of a guilt-ridden man. He must blame to balance his guilt—finding fault and criticizing others in an effort to balance his own guilt. Blame and condemnation are all in the same category. But blame and condemnation do not eradicate the guilt, depression, and loneliness. To be successful, we must use our weapons through God to destroy that stronghold. I have a reason for spending so much time explaining these things to you. I want you to understand how broken relationships work. I also want to motivate you to take action. It's up to you to act. As you act through God's divine power, strongholds will fall. Many people burdened with strongholds of Satan in their lives have learned what to do but are not motivated to act."

Searing the Conscious Mind

Speaking lies destroys a person's ability to think logically and rationally. It prevents the process of "let this mind be in you which was also in Christ Jesus" (Phil 2:5 NKJV). Our mind is divided into two areas: the conscious and the unconscious.

The conscious part of our mind deals only in reality discovered by our five senses (touch, taste, smell, hearing, and sight) and the revelation from God. The unconscious part of our mind deals in fantasy. We dream (nightmares or daydreaming) in our unconscious mind. Our conscious mind is put to rest while we sleep. When the conscious mind is asleep, all sorts of weird, strange, perverse, unrealistic, gory, and scary things come to us through the active, unconscious mind. These unrealistic dreams seem realistic at the time because the unconscious mind does not possess the capacity to sort out the ridiculous and unreal. When we awaken from sleep, the conscious mind is activated again and begins to kick out and reject the absurd things that were accepted by the unconscious mind. This is why, when trying to remember a dream, we forget it about as fast as we can recall it. The conscious mind is rejecting those unreal thoughts that were accepted in the dream as fact. So our conscious mind becomes a safeguard to prevent hallucinations, daydreams, weird thoughts, and such that are given to us by Satan through our unconscious mind.

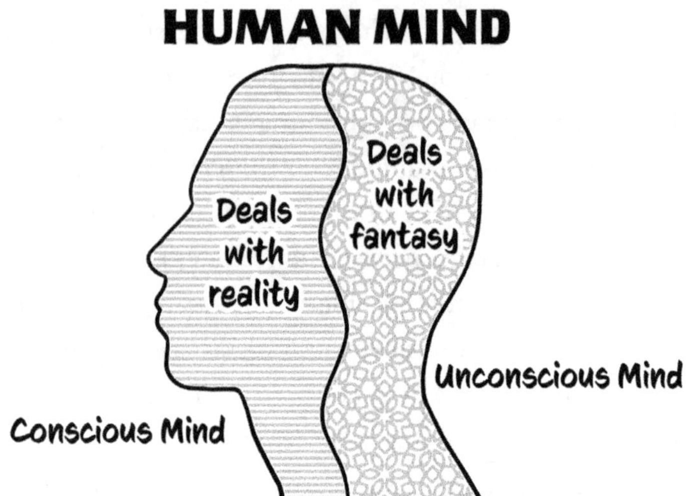

What does all this have to do with searing the conscious mind and Christian living? First Timothy 4:1–2 says, "Now the Spirit expressly says that in later times some will depart from the faith by devoting themselves to deceitful spirits and teachings of demons, through the insincerity of liars whose consciences are seared."

Searing is to make insensitive, as I once discovered when I put my finger on a hot stove. Tsss—the flesh was seared. The finger lost its sensitivity. I could stick the seared flesh with a pin. This further injured the finger, but I felt no pain. The pin in the finger was injuring me, but there was no message to tell me to react to avoid this injury. My finger was seared with the hot stove. *Believing the insincerity of liars* also sears the conscious mind with a hot iron. The conscious mind can no longer kick out or reject the fantasy that was accepted by the unconscious mind. Fears, hallucinations, demons, conspiracy, perverted sexual desires, dreams, and violent acts that have no reality become torment in everyday life.

I will never forget standing in an Oregon jail cell watching an inmate. He was screaming and yelling and in a state of terror. "The snakes are getting me! Get them off my neck!" He was pulling and clawing at his neck, tearing his flesh with his nails. "There are no snakes," I reported to him in sympathy. He could not hear but only continued to fight the imaginary snakes that his unconscious mind said were there. Somehow with alcohol, lies, or believing doctrines of devils he had seared his conscious mind. His God-given safeguard was seared and of little use to him now. That is a terrible way to live. I will never forget the sympathy and helplessness I felt for this man. Believing the lies of the enemy destroys the God-given safeguard of the conscious mind. The garbage comes right on through.

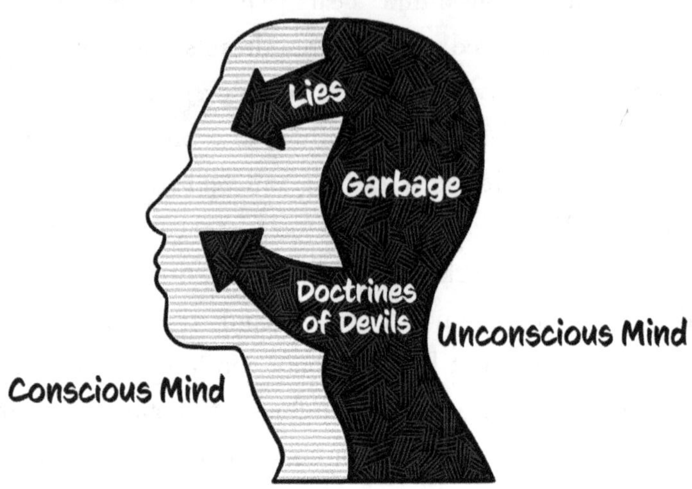

How do we come to believe in these lies? Here are a few examples:

A. There is a popular "faith confession" heretical teaching that says *confess and you will have.* By your confession, God will supply the physical result. For example, "Bless God. I have a new airplane. It is mine. I can see it. I can see myself flying all over the world in it." There, of course, is no airplane. He has no airplane. He is not flying all over the world in it. He is believing the insincerity of liars that begins to sear his conscious mind. Fantasy and unreality begin to sneak through and become mixed with daylight (conscious) activity.

If believing lies continues, this so-called "faith-man" becomes a "fantasy-man."

B. There is a belief that the end justifies the means. Some Christians believe and practice the art of exaggerating miracles, stretching stories, or making up lies to excuse their behavior, all in the name of winning a soul. The lies (the means) are justified by the winning of a soul (the end). This Christian is paying a high price for his "end justifies the means" philosophy. You see, he is believing the insincerity of liars and thus searing his own conscious mind. He is destroying the very thing that God provided for him to *root out* the garbage that comes into his thinking. Is it any wonder that preachers, pastors, ministers, counselors, and Christians find their ministry unfruitful and unrewarding? The spirit of bitterness, the spirit of criticism, and the spirit of fear become constant companions in later years.

C. There is the philosophy that lies are okay as long as they are white lies. A notion is going about the world of psychology and even Christianity that it is acceptable to tell a person a little lie to make him feel good or ease the pain of facing up to reality. The Bible says to speak the truth in love. A lie, whether black or white, small or large, given with good motives or not, is a lie and will sear the conscience of the person speaking the lie. As a counselor, don't be hesitant to divulge the truth and effect of lies upon the mind to the person who is indulging in such activity. Note that the Scriptures tell of a second way the conscious mind may become seared: devoting themselves to deceitful spirits and teachings of demons. Deuteronomy 18:10 mentions horoscopes, fortune tellers, mediums, and other such practices that sear the conscious mind. The fantasy and torment of unreal thoughts plague the life of people who are active in such things. Stay simple in matters of evil, and speak the truth.

D. Speaking lies to rationalize and justify someone's conduct is prevalent in the world. Counselors are tempted to speak lies to ease guilt, to take the blame off the shoulders of the person with the guilt—no matter what the cost. As a Christian counselor, please do not fall into this trap. Those who have tried this method of therapy to ease guilt bear witness that the end is worse than the beginning. Facing the truth is painful, but the long-term result of accepting responsibility for actions truthfully is worth the "ouch" that comes when that "tooth" is pulled.

"So whoever knows the right thing to do and fails to do it, for him it is sin" (James 4:17). Knowledge alone is of little value. But act on that knowledge, and it becomes wisdom. Deal wisely in the affairs of life. Proverbs says that wisdom has more market value than silver and gold. A good way to invest in your future is to gain wisdom. Putting action to your knowledge produces wisdom. The only way to capture a man is to get him to think like you do. Ideas capture men. Win a man's mind, and you have him. Capture his thoughts, and you control him.

Man is a product of this thinking. Early in his public life, Adolph Hitler learned that man is a product of his thinking. Get a man to hate, fear, condemn, and not forgive with you, and that man becomes a *slave of the stronghold.* Hitler's propaganda was designed to enslave people by changing their thinking. "Hate the Jews. Hate the Jews. They are inferior," he declared. On and on he went until the German people were thinking like him. Hate and unforgiveness are a result of broken relationships. They are a stronghold in the mind of a man that will enslave him. He cannot escape. Every place he goes he must take the enslavement with him. The stronghold follows into every area of life.

Chapter 6

Effects of Broken Relationships

Thursday at 11:40 a.m. Tom became angry with his employer, Ernie, and stormed off the job. Tom found other employment and still will not speak to Ernie. Tom has a broken relationship with Ernie. If Tom allows this broken relationship to remain, he can expect to begin seeing evidence of the *effects of broken relationships* in his life. What are the effects?

1. Tom's *wisdom* will begin to deteriorate. He will, over the months and years to come, experience decisions where he more frequently makes the wrong choices. Wisdom is defined as the correct action applied to existing knowledge. Tom may retain his knowledge, but the correct action applied to the knowledge will decrease. If this broken relationship is allowed to exist for a sustained

period of time, Tom can expect to make many costly, embarrassing blunders in the years ahead. Read 1 John 2:9–10.

2. The second effect of the broken relationship for Tom is the *loss of prosperity* and the *loss of answers to his prayers.*

   And whatever we ask we receive from him [God], because we [Tom] keep his commandments and do what pleases him. And this is his commandment, that we believe in the name of his Son Jesus Christ and love one another, just as he has commanded us. Whoever keeps his commandments abides in God, and God in him. And by this we know that he abides in us, by the Spirit whom he has given us.

   —1 John 3:22–24

   Maintaining a life with having no broken relationships and getting your prayers answered are often synonymous. There is a balance between no broken relationships and answered prayer.

As Tom breaks his relationship with Ernie, he upset the balance scale, and answered prayers begin to decrease. I do not define prosperity as money, property, position, or power. Ownership of such things usually does not spell prosperity. In fact, the reverse is usually true. The more money, power, influence, position, and property a man has, the less he is prosperous. H. L. Hunt, the deceased billionaire from Dallas, Texas, said "A man is not prosperous if he knows how much money and property he owns." What I mean by prosperity is righteousness (right relationships with God, others, and self), peace, and joy in the Holy Spirit. Broken relationships destroy this peace and joy, and fellowship with God and others.

3. The third effect Tom can expect from his broken relationship is a deterioration in his *health*. All men are made in the image of God and are not designed to harbor and absorb un-God-like activity such as broken relationships. "Then God said, "Let us make man in our image, after our likeness. . . . So God created man in his own image" (Gen. 1:26–27). Most of our body is run by our automatic control center in our brain (automatic nervous system). This center automatically controls our heart. You do not have to tell your heart to beat. It would be ridiculous to have to say,

"Beat, heart. Come on, beat again and again." All our vital organs—heart, lungs, kidneys, stomach, colon, glands, and so on—are controlled by this automatic control center in our brain.

God also built within us God-like creatures an automatic self-healing system. You cut your finger, and this automatic self-healing system immediately begins to take action to send out corpuscles that kill germs and other necessary action to begin healing the cut. The flu, bacteria, and a host of other germs and diseases are on your skin—possibly in your food—yet you don't get sick. Why? Your automatic self-healing system is working for you, provided you follow God's system of balanced living with no broken relationships. This might be an absurd-sounding thought, but if we believe that every word of the Bible is true, then it is true. To allow a broken relationship in a God-like creature such as Tom (or the rest of us) is like sabotaging a very delicate instrument.

The thoughts that accompany a broken relationship adversely affect the automatic control system. Stress, anxiety, guilt, nervousness, and other such emotions that accompany broken relationships upset the internal organs and reduce health and longevity. We are mind, body, and spirit. The three work closely together. Illness often follows broken relationships. The medical world is discovering that more than 50 percent of all illnesses are directly related to our emotions. The emotions of a person are controlled in part by the effects of broken relationships. Do you want to be healthy? Don't tolerate broken relationships in your life.

4. The fourth effect of broken relationships is a loss of *friends*. It's not much fun to be around people who are experiencing the misery of a broken relationship. They criticize, they complain, they gripe, and they cast blame on others. A spirit of gloom and bad news follows them, pushing away potential friends. They often transfer the hurt from the broken relationship into other relationships. Remember the relationship dynamic between Mr. A, Mr. B, and Mr. X?

5. The fifth effect of broken relationships is a failure to *mature*. A person tends to stay childlike and locked in at the age he was at the time of the broken relationship. Suppose a ten-year-old girl is abused or neglected. That may imprison part of her so she has difficulty maturing and will often cry and behave like a ten-year-old even after marriage twenty-five years later. She can't seem to grow past that stage. Steps to free such a person from this condition will be demonstrated later in this book.

"Mr. Keene, I had no idea broken relationships were so significant," Sandra responded. "I've been so busy concerning myself with everyday life that I haven't learned some of these things. Wow! I am becoming motivated to act on this. But how? I am sorry I interrupted, please go on."

"People with serious broken relationships often can think of little else but that broken relationship. They are continually justifying their own acts. They are continually finding fault with the person with whom they have the broken relationship. It's not much fun to be around people who are so blame-oriented, who criticize and complain about places, every circumstance, and every person in their life. We need to learn to respond correctly to hurts and wrongs done to us."

Sitting on a Tack

"When I was in the third grade at the age of nine," I told Sandra, "I was sabotaged by someone who put a thumbtack on my seat. As soon as I sat down, I felt pain. I was hurt. I had two choices. Number one, I could sit there and continue to experience the pain. Number two, I could get off the tack and stop the continual injury to my bottom. As a third grader, I chose number two. Get off the tack. If you have something going on in your life that is functioning like a tack and is causing pain, *get off the tack*! Get rid of the issue. Be as smart as a third grader."

"Yes, I see that now, Mr. Keene. But what about real

serious wrongs done to a person? What about wrongs that hurt so bad you can't forgive even if you try. What about those? Like my former boyfriend lying to me about marriage and manipulating me just to get privileges. How do I get this unforgiveness out so I can effectively relate to my husband today?" Sandra asked. Sandra was now ready to proceed.

"Alright. Let's go to the third step."

Step Number 3: Ask God's forgiveness for your reaction, and ask God to help you forgive.

"Do you remember the verse in 2 Corinthians 10:4 that said, 'For the weapons of our warfare are not of the flesh but have divine power to destroy strongholds'? God will back us up if we submit to him and seek his assistance. Jesus was and is a healer. He healed the sick, the lame, the blind, and the deaf, and He delivered people who had need and would humbly submit to Him. The Bible says in Psalm 34:18, 'The Lord is near to the brokenhearted.' He will be near to you now with the hurt you still feel from that old relationship. Jesus is the same yesterday, today, and forever. I call this 'Healing the Hurts.' As an act of your will, do you forgive Buddy for the way he wronged you?" I asked Sandra.

Hurt Tapes

IBM computers used to have large magnetic tapes used to store and read data sequentially, serving as an early form of digital memory before modern hard drives and cloud storage. Your mind is like that giant IBM computer. It records everything that happens to you. Events are recorded whether you realize it in your consciousness or not. If you were abused or hurt by someone as a child and that injury has not been healed, your mind can rerun the IBM tape of that hurt over and over again. Unless there is a healing of the hurt, the hurt tape will re-run hundreds and thousands of times during the course of your lifetime. Each time the hurt tape is rerun it hurts anew.

Often hurt tapes create more pain in later life than the pain of the original injury—hurt tapes created by father and stepfather who abused you, people who spoke harshly to you. Hurt tapes created by the neglect and rejection of a person in responsibility such as a teacher or guardian. Hurt tapes created by the love-failure of classmates in school such as people belittling, making fun, ridiculing, and harassing you. People excluding you unfairly. Many hurt tapes are created in teenage years by boyfriend or girlfriend relationships, as in Sandra's case. Hurt tapes are often parent-child love failure. Many hurt tapes are created in later life by abuse, neglect, and cruelty within the marriage. Many people carry hurt tapes from one marriage to another. The hurt needs to be healed. Taking the hurt out of the hurt tape does not eradicate the memory of the incident, but it no longer "hurts" to think about it again. The hurt tape becomes only a tape of little or no consequence to you.

Most people you encounter have hurt tapes that need healing. In a counseling environment, it is often necessary to deal with them first as was done with Sandra. When some of the most prevalent hurts are healed, the person can then begin to successfully deal with the development of a disciplined life that leads to establishing peace, joy, and righteousness here on earth. Putting off the old man (old unsuccessful behavior patterns) and putting on the new man (new response patterns to crisis) then becomes meaningful. *Cumulative hurts* are hurts piled upon hurt until the person hurt becomes insensitive to life. They will not and cannot show much emotion. They lose the ability to express how they feel. They may become numb. They become Wounded Walkers. The hurts have accumulated. As one hurt is healed, other hurts will be exposed so they too may be healed. See *Repressed Emotions* found later in the book for a technique to expose and resolve cumulative hurts.

"Yes, I do forgive him," Sandra responded quickly. "I'm going to pray in a moment, and Jesus is going to go back in time and heal that love-failure caused by Buddy."

"The Bible tells us in James 5:13–16:

> *Is anyone among you suffering? Let him pray. . . . Is anyone among you sick? Let him call for the elders of the church, and let them pray over him, anointing him with oil in the name of the Lord. And the prayer of faith will save the one who is sick, and the Lord will raise him up. And if he has committed sins, he will be forgiven. Therefore, confess your sins to one another and pray for one another, that you may be healed. The prayer of a righteous person has great power as it is working.*

"Sandra, the Bible tells us that the spirit of a man will endure sickness, 'but a crushed spirit who can bear?' That is Proverbs 18:14. Your spirit is hurt. It needs to be healed so your spirit can sustain everyday problems as they come along. A healthy spirit can sustain tremendous problems. A wounded spirit can sustain very little. People who get irritated easily often have a wounded spirit. You have confessed your fault of resentment that still hurts your spirit. This may seem unorthodox, but I would like to obey the verse I just read to you and anoint you with oil in the name of the Lord."

"Yes, please do. I need to be healed," Sandra answered.

Cloetta handed me the small bottle of oil. I removed the tiny lid, spilled a few drops on my finger, and gently applied it to Sandra's head, just above her eyes. It trickled a little and ran slowly down on her face. "Take my hands, Sandra. Let me gently hold both of them. You see, I can tell what is going on inside you through your hands. Relax, Sandra. Just relax. Enter into a state of physical, mental, and spiritual rest. You have done all you can do. You have, as an act of your will, forgiven him. Now relax and submit so Jesus can do His part to destroy that stronghold inside you. Let Him heal your spiritual injury."

I paused to let Sandra relax and then continued. "When we rest from our own works, we can enter into God's rest. Hebrews Chapter 4 tells us that faith does not operate within us until our work stops and we rest. A non-swimmer child cannot be saved from drowning unless he stops struggling. A person cannot heal the hurt of a broken relationship until they surrender it to the Lord. Relax and let the Lord take the hurt away. Jesus will heal you. Sometimes He heals instantly; sometimes He heals slowly over the next several weeks. But nevertheless, He will heal you if you believe and trust Him. Do you believe the Lord is going to heal that hurt for you, Sandra?"

"Yes," she replied in a whisper. Through her hands, I could feel her relaxing. I could almost feel the peace move into her spirit.

"Do you submit yourself to Jesus and trust him, Sandra?"

"Yes," she replied.

"As I start praying, listen to my words intently. As I pray, you agree because Matthew 18:19 says, 'If two of you agree on earth about anything they ask, it will be done for them by my Father in heaven.' Cloetta bowed her head and began to pray softly as I began:

> *Father in the name of Jesus, I ask you to enter into the very spirit of my sister, Sandra, and heal that hurt. Jesus, you are the same yesterday, today, and forever. You were there when this hurt was created, the love-failure that created this hurt. You saw it, and we ask you now to heal her, Lord. Supply your perfect love, Jesus, so there will be no love-failure, so there will be no hurt. Jesus, Sandra and I both forgive Buddy for his failure. We ask that you also forgive him. Thank you, Lord, for your faithfulness to me as I submit my entire life to you. Forgive me for harboring bitterness and unforgiveness toward Buddy. Lord Jesus, I receive your healing this very moment. Praise God! Thank you, Lord. Hallelujah!*

Sandra was trembling. As she sobbed, I knew a healing was taking place. With tears rolling down her face, she looked up with a new fire and sparkle in her eyes. Her cheeks were a healthy rose color. She appeared to glow all over. She looked like an angel. I asked her, "Sandra, can you hear me?" She smiled and nodded her head with one deliberate gesture. "Can you talk?" I added. She replied in a mellow drawn-out fashion, "Yes . . ." "Is the hurt gone? Did the Lord heal you?" I asked.

"Mr. Keene, while you were talking before the prayer about the weapons, our mind, and our broken relationships do you know what I discovered?"

I responded by shaking my head no.

"I discovered I had a broken relationship with Richard, my husband. I had not forgiven him for the way he rejected me. So while you prayed, I also asked the Lord to heal that hurt and love-failure. And do you know what?"

Again, I responded with a negative gesture. I knew but in no way wanted to ruin the joy she was about to share.

"He did heal me. He healed me of both hurts from both men. Oh, Mr. Keene, I am just bursting with love—love for the Lord for healing my hurts, but especially love for my husband. I can hardly wait to get my hands on him. Praise the Lord!"

Chapter 7

Confessing the Wrong

Confession is the only way to eradicate guilt. Blame will not do it. Don't try to shift the blame to others. When a man's folly brings his way to ruin, his heart rages against the Lord.

It is man's own choices that ruin his life, yet he is bitter against the Lord. It is important to understand that bitterness, disappointment, sorrow, and misery come from our own choices. Other people do not make us bitter and miserable, regardless of what they do to us. It is our problem from our incorrect response to their actions. By responding incorrectly, we hurt ourselves. And yet man, in his rebellion, rages against others, lashing out with blame while excusing himself. But ever since Adam and Eve, he has also raged against the Lord.

When God confronted Adam with his disobedience, Adam declared, "The woman whom you gave to be with me, she gave me the fruit of the tree, and I ate" (Gen. 3:12). The woman then shifted the blame to the serpent. The fact that others have done much to shape our lives is a fact. However, everyone must bear personal responsibility for how he allows others to influence his conduct. No one can blame others for his bad behavior, even when he has been taught that behavior from childhood. What he learned may need to be unlearned as he reshapes himself.

We are responsible to confess our faults and allow Jesus to heal these hurts and assist us in reshaping our lives. *The spirit* of a man is continually crying out, "Confess, confess, confess so that I might be healed." *The mind* of that same man says, "Don't confess, don't confess, don't confess. You'll make a fool of yourself and suffer consequences." Paul describes this battle between the mind (the flesh) and the spirit in Romans 7 and 8. Confession ministers to the spirit of a man. That is why a person feels so good in his spirit when he confesses and gets his wrongful behavior off his chest. That is the reason a polygraph (lie detector) works.

The spirit inside will not tolerate a lie without reacting. That reaction can be detected in body functions (heartbeat, perspiration, etc.).

Sandra has confessed her fault of unforgiveness toward her old boyfriend, Buddy. We have prayed and anointed with oil and can expect Sandra to receive a spiritual healing of her hurt. This hurt has been the root of many of Sandra's frustrations. She tells of explosive anger. She tells of anxiety and despair. The root cause is the hurt by Buddy and Richard.

"I'm happy for you, Sandra. The Lord has healed the love-failures and taken the hurt away. You feel very joyous. You are excited about your healing. But listen to me carefully. The excitement will subside in time. You need to know the other steps to assist you as Satan attempts to suggest that you are not healed. Are you ready for step number four?"

Step Number 4: Forgive yourself for harboring bitterness.

I moved back to my chair. "Women are very guilt-prone. Being a woman, Sandra, you are subject to this more than a man. Of course, men feel guilt, too, but women feel guilty more easily than men do. The susceptibility of women to feel guilt is often used by men to manipulate them. I have seen women by the dozens come into my office for divorce. Many of them said to me early in our conversations, 'It's all my fault.' Upon inquiry, I found the husband was drinking heavily, not working, coming home drunk, chasing other women, and at the same time telling his wife, 'It's all your fault.'

"She soon examined herself so closely that she found a weakness. She then accepted the fault cast upon her by her husband. She convinced herself that she was at fault. After all, her husband declared it so, and she could see where she was at fault. She now has guilt. She is miserable. I learned at the age of four that women have an easy inclination to feel guilt. One cold afternoon my parents would not let me go outside. I wanted my own way. I looked at my father and said, 'If you don't let me go outside, I'm going to run away!' Dad simply stated, 'You'll get cold and hungry and soon come home.' He went back to reading his book. I then turned to my mother and said, 'If you don't let me go outside, I'm going to run away!' She looked sad and worried, so I added, 'And the mean old lion will get me and eat me up. Then you'll be sorry! It'll be your fault I'm dead.' A tear came to her eye. She reached down, picked me up, and said, 'It's okay, little Leonard, you can go outside. Get your coat, and I'll help you put it on.' I grinned, scurried for my coat, and then headed outside having found the door to getting my own way with a woman. Cast guilt on them, and you can get anything you want. It was not until I was a little older that I discerned that the guilt I cast on a woman, whether it was my mother, my sister, my friend, or my wife, is to the injury of that woman. Women can't and shouldn't take this guilt. They must learn to dispose of guilt, or they will burst.

"I have since learned to guard my conduct so I will not injure women using guilt as a tool, especially against my wife. 'Likewise, husbands, live with your wives in an understanding way, showing honor to the woman as the weaker vessel, since they are heirs with you of the grace of life, so that your prayers may not be hindered' (1 Peter 3:7). The wife has a more delicate spirit. Every thought and word carries so much weight for her. She will burst if she gets too full of guilt, hurt, or loneliness. How does a woman empty her vessel? As the vessel builds up pressure, it must vent itself to prevent exploding. A woman needs to talk regularly. She needs to confess her shortcomings to her husband so her spirit can feel at peace. If her husband does not listen, she is more susceptible to the deceiving tongue and listening ears of a scoundrel whose sole desire and aim is to steal her attention from her husband and get her into his bed (we will talk more about the role of the husband later). The guilt from wrongful conduct (anything from lying to adultery) rests the heaviest on the women. Sandra, realize that you are guilt-prone and that you need to regularly eradicate any guilt. A good way to forgive yourself is to step up to a large mirror at home. Look yourself straight in the eye and say, 'Sandra, will you forgive me for harboring bitterness against Richard and Buddy?' Then answer, 'Yes, Sandra, I forgive you.' Confess your fault to your husband so you can acquire a good self-image—the I-accept-you-Sandra attitude."

Humility and Self-Image

There is a relationship between humility and a good self-image. As we increase humility on the scale, we also increase our own good image of self. What is humility?

It is being known for what I am and not being ashamed or arrogant about it. It's letting people look at the inside of me. It's letting people see I have weaknesses and hurts inside just like everyone else. As I expose my insides, I also expose my goals and motives. When I open up, I have to clean up selfish and evil motives. I must give up "making myself a big deal." People often refuse to open up and be humble because they fear exposure of their wrong motives, hurts, and weaknesses. This concept needs to be explained to that person. Truth given in love is a mighty force in counseling. Open your hearts to God and others. You can be the example in the new openness. Ephesians 5:21 says, "Submitting yourselves one to another out of reverence for Christ."

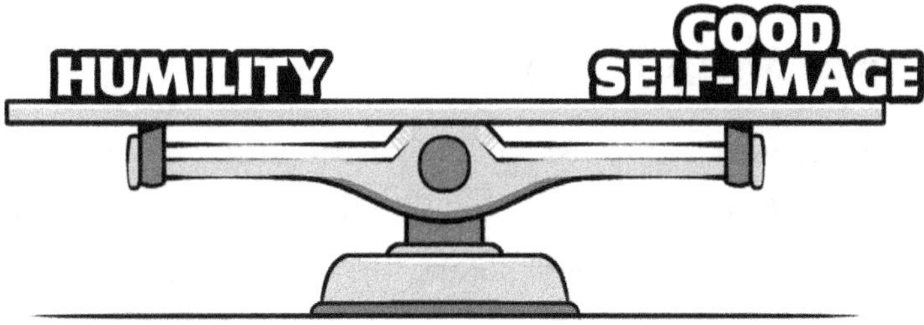

"Sandra, now don't concern yourself again with that former condemnation of self. Forgive yourself and be done with it. Any questions on that point?"

Sandra shook her head no as she looked up from her writing.

"Okay, it's time for step number five."

Step Number 5: Confess out loud: "I forgive ____ (insert the name of the person you need to forgive)."

Counselors Are Examples

A counselor's life must be in correct order to administer truth to others. As my son Randy once reminded me, "Dad, your action speaks louder than your words." Many ministries are not fruitful because their homes are not in order. You must lead well at home first before you can lead elsewhere. With an unloved, neglected, emotionally abused wife at home, rebellious children and finances in a mess, the so-called counselor begins to tell the Wounded Walker how to live successfully. The Wounded Walker can see through this smoke screen of pretended qualities and declares to himself, "No thanks, Mr. Counselor. If your advice is not working in your own life, it probably won't work for me. Besides, I believe I have fewer problems than you."

> *This is why I left you in Crete, so that you might put what remained into order, and appoint elders in every town as I directed you—if anyone is above reproach, the husband of one wife, and his children are believers and not open to the charge of debauchery or insubordination. For an overseer, as God's steward, must be above reproach. He must not be arrogant or quick-tempered or a drunkard or violent or greedy for gain, but hospitable, a lover of good, self-controlled, upright, holy, and disciplined. He must hold firm to the trustworthy word as taught, so that he may be able to give instruction in sound doctrine and also to rebuke those who contradict it.*
>
> —Titus 1:5–9

Jesus preached and showed the Kingdom of God in Luke 8:1. Jesus spoke and demonstrated by his orderly and controlled life the goodness of the Kingdom of God. People could see the Kingdom of God (peace, joy, and righteousness) on the inside of Jesus. His words carried life. Do your words carry life to wounded people? It is time we clean up our act and look like Christians, act like Christians, and experience our inheritance like Christians. Let the wounded people come into your home to see how well you have these principles working in your life. Matthew 7:16 says, "You will recognize them by their fruits." Let us be a people who are recognized by our fruits.

Step Number 6: Ask forgiveness from those you have wronged or hurt.

Is there a stumbling block in the path of one of your former acquaintances because of you? Does someone hate or dislike you? Does someone hold resentment toward you? A direct confrontation is necessary. Phone calls or emails seldom work adequately. Matthew 5:23–24 says. "So if you are offering your gift at the altar and there remember that your brother has something against you, leave your gift there before the altar and go. First be reconciled to your brother, and then come and offer your gift." Your gifts to God in the form of money, property, time, talent, or praise are of little consequence if you have a broken relationship with another person.

It is no small wonder that so many ministries bear bad fruit. They have not cleaned up their past relationships. Husband and wife are arguing and fighting on the way to church. As they put on their painted-on smile at the church door, the broken relationship is still in their hearts. Why doesn't God honor my worship? Why doesn't God honor my gifts of praise, money, and time? Man cannot love God and hate man. If you truly love God, you will mend all broken relationships. If you do this, your gifts at the altar will be meaningful.

I knew a man who had a broken relationship with a coworker. They faced one another every day but would not speak or let their eyes meet. This went on for six years. Finally, one of the men moved away. As far as I know, both men are still enslaved with this broken relationship. I have seen that asking forgiveness for your wrongful conduct usually will be returned with a statement similar to this: "Oh, you should be the one forgiving me. I wronged you badly. I should be the one asking forgiveness."

"Sandra, in your case, you would be ill-advised to seek out the old boyfriend. Don't reactivate that relationship by returning to him. The Lord has healed you. You can pray for him so the Lord can begin to help him. However, you should go to your husband and ask forgiveness for your attitude toward him. That will help make your husband more sensitive to your delicate spirit. Even though you were only

5 percent at fault, still ask his forgiveness. Make sure you follow the commandment of Ephesians to speak the truth in love—not the truth in bitterness. Read and study all of Matthew Chapter 18. Make certain you and the Lord have purged out all the bitterness."

Sandra spoke up with a quick "Why?"

"Because bitterness can be tasted by the other person. Bitterness is in its very nature bitter! It turns people away. Make certain your speech has no bitterness, your actions have no bitterness, and particularly your attitude has no bitterness. Guilt, depression, loneliness, and bitterness all show up in one or more of these three places: our speech, our actions, or our attitude."

Chapter 8
Spiritual Cover

Often a person's problem stems from a failure to understand and maintain spiritual cover. A family needs a husband in authority and a wife in submission to keep the wolf away. The parable of the hundred sheep in Matthew 18, starting in verse 12, demonstrates this. The wolf strategically goes after the one lone sheep who by his rebellious nature wanders off from the protection of the fold—thus vulnerable to attack. The parable tells us the shepherd follows the lone sheep. I can almost visualize the shepherd taking his crooked cane and beating the wolf away from that lonely sheep. The wolf bites at the heels and snaps at the ears of the lone sheep. The shepherd pleads for the sheep to resubmit to the fold. The shepherd says, "Please come back with me. You'll be safe and protected there."

You see, the submitted relationships of the sheep in the fold protect each one of them from Satan, who goes about as a roaring lion seeking someone to devour (1 Pet. 5:8). "Mr. Lone Sheep, please submit yourself to the fold. Don't be afraid. I will protect you." Submission requires the lone sheep to be humble toward the other sheep. 1 Peter 5:5 says to be clothed with humility. This clothing of humility protects and covers each sheep in the fold from the wolf and the lion.

In my experience as a counselor, most people in need of guidance and help fit into the lone sheep class. What are the reasons for leaving the fold? They range from greed and selfishness to hurt and injury—from greed for self to hurts from other sheep. It is the counselor's responsibility to motivate the lone sheep to return to the fold. I have found the most successful way to motivate is to explain this concept of entering into close relationship again. People get weak and weary from the harassment of the wolf. It is then that we must be bold and rescue them with truth—the truth that sets us free from the bondage of doing our own thing. "Humble yourselves before the Lord, and he will exalt you" (James 4:10). How do I humble myself before God? Humble yourself in the fold by submitting and subjecting to other followers of Christ. By doing so, you have automatically humbled yourself to God. It is then that God's grace begins to give you spiritual cover and protection. Open yourself to one another. Enter into close relationships with one another. Bring everything out into the light. Invest in your spiritual family.

> *Likewise, you who are younger, be subject to the elders. Clothe yourselves, all of you, with humility toward one another, for "God opposes the proud but gives grace to the humble. Humble yourselves, therefore, under the*

mighty hand of God so that at the proper time he may exalt you, casting all your anxieties on him, because he cares for you. Be sober-minded; be watchful. Your adversary the devil prowls around like a roaring lion, seeking someone to devour.

—1 Pet. 5:5–8

"Sandra, the Lord tells wives to submit to their husbands as to the Lord. To submit means 'to open your arms' to receive the love from the husband—to fit into the husband's plans, to adapt yourself to him. Sandra, open your arms. Stretch them out wide. Notice that all your vital organs are exposed—your face, your heart, your stomach, your lungs, and your reproductive organs. When a woman submits to her husband, she exposes these vital organs to him. When a husband fails to love his wife correctly, he injures her.

"When a husband rejects his wife, it is much like the husband taking a knife and stabbing her in the vital organs. What happens when your arms are open in a submitted stance and someone slugs you in the stomach? Your arms immediately close. It hurts. Your arms close to protect yourself. That is what a wife does when a husband abuses, neglects, or rejects her. A love-failure on the husband's part injures the submitted wife. She begins to close her arms for protection. Continued abuse, neglect, and rejection will close her arms of submission until she is no longer able to submit. When a wife is not in submission with open arms, she cannot receive love. There are too many hurts. 'I can't trust him.' What you have been doing, Sandra, is learning about these things and allowing the Lord to heal those love-failures so you can once again open your arms in submission to your husband. Love will pass by if the intended receiver is not in the correct submitted stance. Let's draw a picture of the submission."

I went to the chalkboard and began to draw as I explained.

Glancing at Cloetta, I walked back to my chair. Cloetta motioned toward the coffee pot, and I nodded yes. As she refilled my cup and Sandra's, I went on talking. "Sandra, keep your spiritual arms of submission open long enough for your husband to love you."

Often it becomes a matter of teaching a husband to love his wife. Many husbands do not realize the complexity involved in loving their wife. Loving your wife is more than just having intimacy with her on occasion and bringing money home to pay bills. A woman must be loved twenty-four hours a day, not just thirty minutes occasionally. Loving her includes closing the computer and turning off the television to listen to her talk about her day and things regarding the home and the children. Women need quality conversation. A husband needs to learn to be a good listener to allow his wife to empty her "vessel" so it will not burst.

Loving your wife means spending intentional time with her on Saturday rather than golfing with your best friend. A man truly becomes a man when he makes his wife his best friend, continually wooing and loving her in small things. Mowing the grass, fixing the house, and taking out the trash are all interpreted by women as an expression of love. Now comes the hard truth for husbands. Whose responsibility is it to see that the husband-and-wife relationship stays intact? Some say it is both the husband's and the wife's. They say the husband and wife share equal responsibility to keep the marriage intact. Well, in a way I suppose that is true. But this usually ends with both husband and wife blaming one another for not pulling their load when difficulty arises. Some say it is the woman's responsibility to keep the marriage intact because after all, she is the homemaker. They say it is her job to submit to the husband, and the trouble begins when women fail to submit. But I found this also not wholly correct. Most women want to submit to their husbands. Most women do submit to their husbands with "open arms." But men, not knowing how to love their wife correctly or not realizing they should learn to love their wife, have rejected, neglected, and abused her. The wife then pulls back, closes her arms of submission to protect herself, and the marriage becomes nothing more than an arrangement to get the kids raised.

The wife has found she can't trust her husband, so she begins to lead. The wife is now leading the marriage. What was meant to be a display of Christ's role in leading the Church is now backwards. This is not the way God designed it. When the wife is in leadership, husbands want to stay away from the conflict at home, so they play golf, take out-of-town jobs, work extra hours, or worst of all, find another woman to make them "feel like a man." He will do anything to avoid the conflict that occurs at home when the roles of husband and wife are reversed.

I believe it is the husband's responsibility to see that the marriage stays intact. It is his responsibility to see that outsiders and foreign objects (bitterness) do not separate the relationship. It is the husband's job to stop a wild beast from attacking the marriage—to stop anything that might divide the husband-wife relationship. It was Adam's sin when he allowed Eve to be deceived by Satan. Adam was held accountable by God. Genesis 2:24 says, "Therefore a man shall leave his father and his mother and hold fast to his wife, and they shall become one flesh." The man is always in motion. He is leaving one place and going to another. In the man's relationship, he is always leaving his father and mother and moving toward his wife—moving toward her in a continual effort of pursuit, a pursuit to establish the husband and wife as one flesh. This doesn't happen magically when you say "I do" at the altar. The man must be the aggressor. He is the one who must seek out his wife daily. He must be the aggressor in intimacy, protection, provision, and leading the family.

Chapter 9

The Hurry, Hurry Syndrome

The hurry, hurry syndrome often destroys a person's sensitivity. And of course, sensitivity is a key to effective relationships. In my studies, I've found that people in a hurry are often the people who need counseling and therapy later in life. There is also a need for counseling those people who live around the man or woman in a hurry. Why? They break relationships with other people. Others are offended; others are hurt; others are injured by this man or woman in a hurry. The guilt and effect of the broken relationships show up in later life. It's much like a red Washington delicious apple from Tacoma that you have kicked with your foot and bruised. The bruise is not apparent because the skin of the apple was not broken. But the kick bruised the apple on the inside. For the next few hours, the bruised apple appears to be a healthy Grade A apple. However, with the passing of time, a dark brown and black spot becomes apparent on the surface. If the results of this injury are not cut out and removed, it will soon contaminate and destroy the entire apple. The apple will become useless and of no value.

Much the same thing happens in broken relationships with people. If these broken relationships are not healed, they will contaminate and render useless the people involved. Proverbs 19:2 says, "Whoever makes haste with his feet misses his way." Why? He steps on people and breaks relationships. Man is not constructed by God to run 120 miles per hour continually. If he does, he will soon run out of gas. Heart attacks, ulcers, colitis, respiratory illness, early death, broken marriages, and juvenile delinquencies in children are often the plight of the forty-year-old man in a hurry.

Slow down, men, or you will leave a widow behind. Learn to pace yourself so you can climb the entire mountain. The first time I climbed Mt. Pitt in Southern Oregon I learned this lesson. I was 6 miles from the top. The first 2 miles I almost ran, anxious to conquer the mountain. Our guide said, "Slow down or we'll bury you along the route." We climbed the mountain one step at a time—slowly but surely, never in a hurry, pacing and conserving our energy for the full climb. Husbands, lead your families at a slower pace.

Just as the Lord continually woos man with love, asking for more submission to Him, so a husband must continually woo his wife with love. As she begins to trust him, she slowly opens her arms of submission to him. As she submits, she receives the husband's love. The more the husband woos and loves her, the more she trusts him. As she learns to trust her husband, she opens further her arms of submission to him. "They shall be one flesh," the verse says, and the man "shall cleave unto his wife" (Gen 2:24 KJV). *Cleave* means "to fasten together"—like a button in the buttonhole. The button is not much by itself. Neither is the buttonhole. But as the button actively seeks out the buttonhole and "woos" it into submission, a relationship is established. The button and the buttonhole have become one. They are fastened together.

Husband, cleave to your wife. Fasten yourselves together so no outsider, including bitterness and resentment, can separate this relationship. It is your responsibility. See that the husband-wife relationship is securely cleaved (fastened) together as one flesh. Husband, you are accountable to God as head of your home for the success of the relationship. "What therefore God has joined together, let no man separate" (Matt. 19:6). What therefore God has joined together, let no husband allow to separate. We as husbands are accountable to God for this relationship. It was Adam's sin when he allowed Satan to intervene in the marriage. It will be the husband's sin if he allows a third party or problems to separate the husband-wife relationship.

Reject. Neglect. Abuse: the three enemies of submission, the three things that stop a wife from the "open arms of submission." When the arms of submission close, the wife no longer can receive love from the husband. A vessel must have the lid off in order to receive. A vessel must be submitted to be filled. Rejection, neglect, and abuse put the lid on the vessel. The vessel is no longer submitted. The lid is on the vessel to protect it. It cannot receive the wine. As I pour the wine, it hits the lid and spills down the side—wasted.

"Sandra, the Lord has taken the lid off your vessel so you can receive again the love of your husband. The Lord has healed the love-failure caused by Richard. It was the neglect, the rejection, and the abuse that caused you to close your arms of submission for protection. You couldn't receive the occasional love offered by Richard because you were not submitted. The Lord has healed those love-failures. This healing is a slow process, but as you are healed, spiritual submission will allow you to once again receive love from your husband. Learn to adapt yourself to your husband. Learn to look to him as your shepherd."

"But Mr. Keene, how will Richard learn that a husband's neglect, rejection, and abuse stop a wife's submission? What will stop him from injuring me again?" Sandra asked.

"Sandra, I want you to begin to speak the truth in love toward your husband. Tell him honestly how you feel. Before the Lord healed your injuries, you could not have done this. You would have spoken the truth in bitterness. If there is bitterness and resentment (caused by an injury from neglect, rejection or abusive conduct) in a wife's spirit, the husband can detect it. He can actually taste the resentment. It's bitter. When we eat something that is bitter, we spit it out. That is exactly what a husband does when he tastes the bitterness in his wife's attitude, action, or speech. Even if it is truth, the bitterness coats it. He spits it out by more abuse, more neglect, and more rejection. Sometimes it's by a blow to the head. Sometimes he gets angry. Sometimes he just disappears.

"But Sandra, now the bitterness is gone. You can speak the truth about your feelings to him. You can begin to expose your thoughts. You are beginning a new age of communication to become one flesh. As you express yourself in love toward Richard, he will become more aware of your emotional needs. He will become more sensitive to your desire to submit. Begin to admire him. Men need to be admired by their wives. In due time explain broken relationships to him. Or if you feel led by God, have him come in. Perhaps I can talk with him. He will learn to stop abuse, neglect, and rejection if you begin to speak your feelings to him in love—not just your bad feelings but also your good emotions, particularly your good feelings. Begin to expose your love for him in words, in action, and in attitude. God will now begin to deal with him."

"Mr. Keene, is there anything else I can do to make my husband aware that he needs to love me more intentionally? That he needs to be the one to fasten the relationship together in one flesh?" Sandra asked.

"Read Ephesians Chapter 5 with him. Don't instruct him. Let him lead. The Lord will reveal the truth to him in time. Be patient. You may want to describe this counseling session to him. Resist the temptation. He will begin to see that the Lord has returned you to a submitted position to receive his love. 'Hurry,' the Lord says, 'love her while there is still time. Love her as I loved the church. Love her as I love you. I gave my life at the cross for you.'

"Husbands should also give their everything to their wife, especially their time and attention. If a man earns a million dollars a year in his business and is mayor of the city or president of this and that but is a failure at home, he is a failure in the eyes of God. No man wants to fail. God will show you both how to communicate with one another. Submit yourselves one to another to receive one another's love."

Ephesians 5

Therefore be imitators of God, as beloved children. And walk in love, as Christ loved us and gave himself up for us, a fragrant offering and sacrifice to God. But sexual immorality and all impurity or covetousness must not even be named among you, as is proper among saints. Let there be no filthiness nor foolish talk nor crude joking, which are out of place, but instead let there be thanksgiving. For you may be sure of this, that everyone who is sexually immoral or impure, or who is covetous (that is, an idolater), has no inheritance in the kingdom of Christ and God. Let no one deceive you with empty words, for because of these things the wrath of God comes upon the sons of disobedience. Therefore do not become partners with them; for at one time you were darkness, but now you are light in the Lord. Walk as children of light (for the fruit of light is found in all that is good and right and true), and try to discern what is pleasing to the Lord. Take no part in the unfruitful works of darkness, but instead expose them. For it is shameful even to speak of the things that they do in secret. But when anything is exposed by the light, it becomes visible, for anything that becomes visible is light. Therefore it says,

"Awake, O sleeper,
and arise from the dead,
and Christ will shine on you."

Look carefully then how you walk, not as unwise but as wise, making the best use of the time, because the days are evil. Therefore do not be foolish, but understand what the will of the Lord is. And do not get drunk with wine, for that is debauchery, but be filled with the Spirit, addressing one another in psalms and hymns and spiritual songs, singing and making melody to the Lord with your heart, giving thanks always and for everything to God the Father in the name of our Lord Jesus Christ, submitting to one another out of reverence for Christ.

Wives, submit to your own husbands, as to the Lord. For the husband is the head of the wife even as Christ is the head of the church, his body, and is himself its Savior. Now as the church submits to Christ, so also wives should submit in everything to their husbands.

Husbands, love your wives, as Christ loved the church and gave himself up for her, that he might sanctify her, having cleansed her by the washing of water with the word, so that he might present the church to himself in splendor, without spot or wrinkle or any such thing, that she might be holy and without blemish. In the same way

> *husbands should love their wives as their own bodies. He who loves his wife loves himself. For no one ever hated his own flesh, but nourishes and cherishes it, just as Christ does the church, because we are members of his body. "Therefore a man shall leave his father and mother and hold fast to his wife, and the two shall become one flesh." This mystery is profound, and I am saying that it refers to Christ and the church. However, let each one of you love his wife as himself, and let the wife see that she respects her husband.*

I looked at Cloetta and said, "Could I have one more cup of coffee?" Cloetta smiled, slid out of her chair, and moved toward the doorway as I stood to erase the chalkboard. Then she spoke. "There are pastries in the coffee room. Do either of you want one?" She stood, waiting at the door for our reply.

"Something very small," Sandra said.

Cloetta looked at me. She was sure what my response was going to be. I smiled and nodded in affirmation. As Cloetta left to prepare coffee and pastries, I thought to myself, *We have become so professional in our counseling that we tend to set time limits on each session.* Appointments are scheduled back to back. One-hour or one-and-a-half-hour sessions do not produce much fruit. The client barely gets settled down from the activities and fear of life, and it is time for her to leave. No time to build a relationship, no time to confess faults, no time to forsake bad behavior, no time to anoint and pray, and not enough time to teach how to enter into close relationships with others. Remembering back to the hundreds and hundreds of clients I've counseled, I thought, *The real success cases came from the counseling session when we had unrestricted time allotted to the first session.* Two or four hours in the first session. Then only a few phone calls in follow-up to solidify the results of the session. Although nervous and upset, a person is more open to receive during that initial session. The client has submitted to the counselor, submitted to receive assistance for a problem the client cannot solve. The client has tried everything. Now they need your help. They possibly have talked to people and family, read books, and spent hours in anxiety looking for an answer, all to no avail.

Chapter 10

Fixations

How a person views a situation can be hindered by a "fixation." If a person has a "they will hurt me fixation," he will interpret many situations as a threat to his well-being. The threat is real in his thinking, even though there is no real danger. If I was riding in your car while you were driving and you heard me yell, "Look out for the truck," you would feel threatened if by past experience you had determined that trucks do indeed collide with cars. You have been conditioned to respond to such alarm. This conditioning was established from experience or knowledge imparted to you by other situations.

Many people have a "salvation fixation." They have heard salvation through Jesus so often that they are conditioned to respond with alarm and with a loud "no thanks." The message is a threat to their being. Or, in the case of some Christians who read the Bible with a "salvation fixation," it's interpreting most verses as directing man to heaven. Or other Christians who have a "faith" or "money" fixation read the word *give* in the Bible, and the words money, money, money echo in their minds. Their fixation on money has hindered their ability to discern the Bible verse the way the Lord intended. For example, some people with incorrect motives and goals could easily read Luke 6:38—"Give, and it will be given to you" as meaning money, money, money without giving thought to the fact that *give* is a verb, and you must locate the noun or subject that it is referring to. Without a money fixation, a person can easily go to the previous verse and find out what the writer is referring to when he says "give."

"Be merciful, even as your Father is merciful. Judge not, and you will not be judged; condemn not, and you will not be condemned; forgive, and you will be forgiven" (Luke 6:36–38). The idea is to be merciful, not judge, not condemn, and forgive. It has nothing to do with money or property. In fact, the writer of Luke was a physician, a doctor of his time. He was not a financier or a man of God giving some secret to getting rich. Many people who seek your counsel will have fixations—fixations that hinder their ability to discern life and circumstances. It takes patience and re-education to dispose of these many fixations. A common fixation encountered by counselors is wrong goals. People who love themselves so much believe that all situations in life are analyzed on the basis of "will this benefit me or profit me?" This is a "self-fixation." It often deters genuine friendship and creates selfish, lonely people. The people with self-fixations usually experience frustrations, guilt, and confusion in later years of their life.

The client is at the end of her rope. Desperate. Crying out in a submitted spirit for help. This initial two- to four-hour session is often the best time to get to the problem. Occasionally a few clients receive benefit from the time spent in counseling in future sessions. To understand the reason for this, it is necessary to understand the concept of Ears-to-Hear. "Pay attention to what you hear: with the measure you use, it will be measured to you, and still more will be added to you. For to the one who has, more will be given, and from the one who has not, even what he has will be taken away" (Mark 4:24–25).

A client comes for counseling expecting to receive help, expecting to receive help in a certain area of his life—help to the extent and to the degree they have submitted to the counselor and have Ears-to-Hear. The counselor must discern this area of submission in the client and aim his advice and counsel at that area. It is only in that area that the client has Ears-to-Hear. If the counselor fails to discern that critical area of submission, the client will not receive, no matter how artful and articulate the counselor instructs and guides.

For example, Joann came to me. She was in trouble with the law. There was a warrant out for her arrest for an overdrawn bank account. She wanted help. She submitted to me and had ears to hear concerning solving her legal entanglement. I could detect from her conversation that she had more serious problems. She had several broken relationships that were bothering her. I also could detect that she was over-extended in her activities. She was just too busy—so busy with work, recreation, and friends that she had no time to mentally step aside, stop, and reexamine her life. She needed to stop to see more clearly where she was going and why she was going there. My target area as counselor was to hone in on the area of submission where Joann had ears to hear—her legal problem.

As I began to hit this area with my counsel, her ears to hear were receiving, and much like the verse says, "to the one who has, more will be given." Her area of submission quickly increased so we were able to move into areas of business and broken relationships. If the counselor misses this target area of submission, the client will not receive but often becomes irritated and closes up the small area she had allotted to have ears to hear. A diagram will illustrate this. Some clients arrive at the office totally submitted. They are so desperate that they have ears to hear in all areas. But generally speaking, it starts with the one limited area. As soon as the counselor locates that area and begins to minister, the client learns to trust the counselor. As trust and ears to hear develop and expand into larger areas, the counselor can also expose and cover more of the problem.

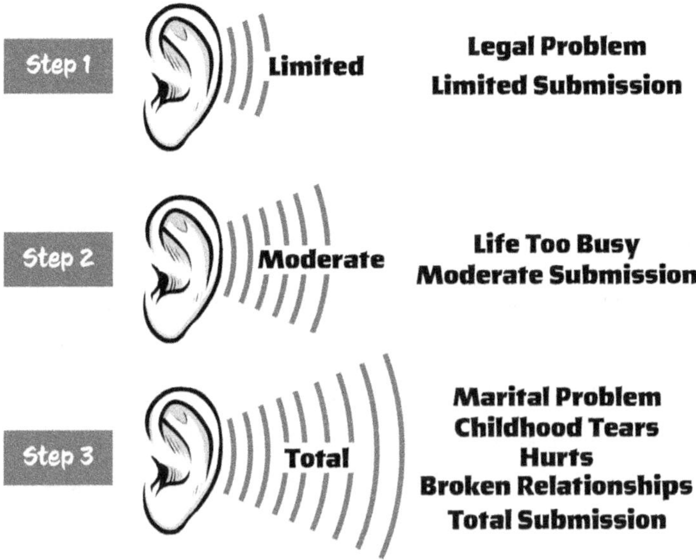

The door opened as Cloetta quickly entered, carrying a tray of coffee and several delicious-looking pastries. There was a spirit of excitement in the air—not just the excitement about coffee and pastry but the excitement of the "light" and the "healing" that was taking place in Sandra's life. I looked at my $10 Timex. It was exactly 4:00 p.m. We had been in conference two hours. Look what progress we had made. I wish all cases would progress at this speed. People need help so badly. So many are suffering at the hands of one another. People continue to suffer because of a fear of more injury if they open up to another human being. There is fear of exposing our hurts, guilt, motives, and weakness. We are ashamed, not knowing whether the person we open up to will stab us in the stomach with a knife or make fun and ridicule our weaknesses. Sandra ate her pastry slowly and deliberately, taking small bites and chewing each piece almost as though her mind was in another world.

Remove Tension-Producers

Headaches, backaches, and confusion are often caused by tension-producers. The television blaring hour after hour can create tension. An environment of troublesome coworkers, a job you hate, an untrustworthy car that irritates can be serious tension-producers. They often destroy happiness and lead to early death. It is often useful in counseling to have the person describe an entire day, hour for hour. After that, have him describe an entire week, day by day. Clues will surface that will identify a problem of overwork, lack of sleep, or wrong employment. They might have an employer who is abusive, a lack of a hobby or diversion, or failure to worship regularly. Don't think counseling has to be so professional and highly introspective that everyday, practical solutions are not used. All problems are not solved by digging deep into the past. The present environment is often the cause and the cure.

We all sat quietly for a few moments, and then Sandra spoke. "I must settle something in my life before I leave here, Mr. Keene. I feel a need to really open up and tell you what I feel on the inside. I feel like you will understand and be able to help me."

"Go ahead and talk, Sandra. Tell me whatever you like. I'm here to help," I replied. As she began to talk, I thought of the submission the Lord was talking about in 1 Peter 5. As we submit to one another, we are clothed (covered) with humility, and the mighty hand of God begins to cover and protect us from Satan who as a roaring lion goes about seeking who he may devour. Satan is looking for the lone sheep, the unsubmitted sheep—the one sheep doing his or her own thing. As the lone sheep gets torn, injured, bit, kicked, and abused, a crusty wall of fear attaches itself to the spirit of that "sheep." The crusty wall of fear prevents outsiders from entering. It also prevents the real you from exposing the weaknesses and hurts inside. This crusty wall of fear around Sandra's spirit has begun to crumble. She now wants to really expose some of her inner hurts and weaknesses. She trusts me not to laugh or further injure her. We have begun building a relationship. The relationship has loyalty and trust as a main ingredient.

Sandra was talking softly. "I have never really thought of myself as having many fears. But I am beginning to see that my worries are really fears. When I worry about something happening to Richard, I can see it really goes back to when I was always afraid something was going to happen to my dad. I always had a hidden fear that one day he might be killed coming home. Where this came from, I really don't know, except maybe from hearing my parents fight. They fought over money or drinking. I knew my dad was a fast driver and did at times mix drinking and driving. One time when my parents were fighting, they called me in and asked who I would choose to stay with. They, of course, did not divorce, and all the trouble, outwardly at least, was soon forgotten. But they failed to pass the news on to us kids. It is confusing as a child to see so much hate, and then see them getting along—sort of like the song 'The Games People Play.' I now see that it is not really a game, but rather hurts. Unless they understand hurts as you have explained them to me, they will be plagued for life. I really see where they, like myself, have to desire the hurt to be removed, seek inner healing, and in my case build a good relationship with my husband. Then and only then, the hurt becomes a remembrance and not pain.

"My parents were good people and I'm sure in no way intentionally hurt us. I always felt second best, even though I was the oldest. My brother was sick a lot, and all the money needed to be spent on him, and all the attention made me want to be sick also. I sort of inwardly thought that someday I'll get sick, and you'll have to baby me. Money was another problem. Someone was always spending too much. I guess that is why I try so hard never to complain about money. I saw how it divided relationships. As a child I was very quiet. I had a speech problem when I started school. At school, the kids would get me to say something and then laugh. Even when I answered roll call, they laughed. They may have been laughing with me; however, I was not laughing. So I just drew back.

"One time in junior high school we were passing around our yearbooks for signatures. I overheard one girl ask whose book she had. The girl next to her answered, 'Oh, the girl that never talks or does anything.' That answer caused me to cry myself to sleep that night and many nights after. It really did hurt because I always thought I was just being polite. Anyway, that thought helped me justify my not talking and not expressing my emotions to others.

"We moved my last year of high school, and I had to talk. The kids in the new school didn't know I was quiet and never talked. They asked questions, and I answered. It was a small school, so there was no getting lost in the crowd. Now I probably talk too much. I still do not like large crowds or totally new crowds. And I do prefer to be in the background. I really believe in the Bible where it says a woman is not supposed to talk in church or teach men. I guess that is why I really want my husband to be the man of the house. I want him strong so I can be behind him, so he will make the decisions, protect me and love me.

"Now I know I don't have to be sick to be loved, talk lots to be loved, or know all about money, news, investments or anything else. I just need to be loved and taken care of, knowing each night that he'll come home. I guess what I really want is to become the one flesh you talked about. I want to have a family someday. And I want them to have good parents, ones they will be proud of. Now that I talk about it, I guess I do have fears. Sometimes I wake up at night trembling. Sometimes I get fearful during the day when I'm alone. I'm afraid the elevator will stick and leave me alone between floors. Mr. Keene, are these fears caused by the things in my childhood? The things I just told you about? I'm an adult now. How can I still be hung up over childhood fears?" She ended with a deep sigh.

Chapter 11

Repressed Emotions

Unlike Sandra, not all clients are willing to express their emotions. In fact, many people find it difficult or impossible to express their inner feelings. We can call these repressed emotions. Here's an illustration. Suppose Alice at four years old is left with the babysitter while Dad and Mom go to a party. Alice is told her parents will return at midnight. At 2:00 a.m. she awakes from sleep and asks the babysitter, "Where is my Daddy and Mommy?" The sitter explains that they have not returned. Alice cries. The sitter tells Alice that "big girls don't cry." She was told not to express the emotion of hurt or disappointment, that it's not grown-up-like.

At 6:00 a.m. Alice again awakes and asks, "Where is my Daddy and Mommy?" The sitter explains again that "Daddy and Mommy have not returned." Alice feels rejected again. She begins to cry and weep again, expressing the hurt that is on the inside. She misses her parents. Her parents lied to her. There is hurt and pain—pain that is almost unbearable, pain that feels like a knife in her stomach. Again, the sitter reminds Alice that "big girls don't cry, so go back to sleep." The implication is that she should not express the hurt that is inside her. Alice can't stop herself. She cries, expressing the hurt uncontrollably. The sitter gets angry and further rejects and rebukes Alice. When Mom and Dad finally do come at 10:00 a.m. Alice runs to them with open arms, crying. Both parents tell her, "Don't cry. We are here now. Be a big girl. Don't cry." Alice learns to repress emotions such as hurt, despair, anger, guilt, and frustration as not being adult. If these emotions are not expressed and dealt with, they are never disposed of.

These unexpressed emotions stay inside Alice and torment her. She begins to accumulate more unexpressed emotions. She represses them. Inside, the fear of exposure mounts up until Alice doesn't dare let anyone see what is on the inside since they may declare her to be childish, weak, or sick. What does Alice do? She closes up and does not allow people to see on the inside. Alice has repressed emotions from hurts. Alice can never truly be happy and enter into peace, joy, and righteousness until these emotions are vented and confronted.

Modern lifestyles demand men and women to be strong, courageous loners and not express emotions. Few people have close relationships in which they can vent their feelings. Remembering that most people who come for counseling are loners, we can begin to see the importance of Step Number 1 in counseling: Develop the relationship. With the hurried lifestyle, there is more need for close relationships than ever before. The most successful method I've found to assist "an Alice" to release these repressed emotions and begin building a relationship with another human being is to use the Sentence Completion Exercise. I present several phrases, the beginning parts of sentences, that the client is to finish with the first words that enter her mind and are a completion of the sentence. When the client expresses a willingness to cooperate, I explain the procedure as follows.

I say the first part of a series of incomplete sentences. As spontaneously and as quickly as possible, the client will reply with the first set of words that occurs to them that complete the sentence. Don't worry about the rightness or wrongness of your response, I tell them. There are no right or wrong answers. The client should avoid editing or censoring their replies. I'm simply interested in the first response that occurs to them. Never mind if the response sounds foolish, ridiculous, illogical, or the exact opposite of their beliefs. They should just relax and not try to make anything happen. They shouldn't try to second-guess or analyze but just let what happens, happen.

Here is an example. I say, "When I look at the mountain," and you might say, "I see snow and trees." Here is a list of incomplete sentences that can be used to get the feelings started.

1. When I get up in the morning . . .
2. As a woman/man . . .
3. Sometimes I feel . . .
4. I don't understand myself when . . .
5. Why do I always . . .
6. Whenever I try . . .
7. I want . . .
8. I can't tolerate . . .
9. Weakness to me means . . .
10. If I give into my feelings . . .
11. When people look at me . . .
12. Why do people so often . . .
13. God is . . .
14. When I look in the mirror . . .
15. Ever since I was a child . . .
16. I feel safe when . . .
17. My mother was always . . .
18. She always expected . . .
19. She never . . .
20. That made me feel . . .
21. And it also made me feel . . .
22. My father was always . . .
23. He never . . .
24. He always expected . . .

We can never feel forgiveness for an emotion we will not admit having. It is difficult to confess to God an emotion we do not confess to ourselves. This test will assist people who have not been accustomed to venting emotions or facing up to them.

25. When I made a mistake . . .
26. Men/women (opposite sex) are . . .
27. Men/women (same sex) are . . .
28. Being alone to me means . . .
29. Pleasure to me is . . .
30. Freedom to me means . . .
31. If I ever let out my anger . . .
32. I don't dare show my anger because . . .
33. Sometimes I push my thoughts away because . . .
34. Sometimes I want to cry out . . .
35. Sometimes I feel guilty when . . .
36. The thing I'm most tired of is . . .
37. To me, worship is . . .
38. If I were to be more emotionally vulnerable . . .
39. It's hard to be open because . . .
40. Being hurt means . . .
41. If I ever admitted I needed someone . . .
42. I cut myself off from people because . . .
43. When I admit that I love someone . . .
44. To submit means . . .
45. I can remember . . .
46. Committing myself means . . .
47. I can't do that because . . .
48. If I didn't always have to protect myself . . .

This is not an exhaustive list of phrases, and you can add to it as the client opens up to you in areas of concern. As they begin to confess and express the repressed feelings and emotions, they will find they can more adequately confront their problem. It is often useful to record your counseling sessions and let the client take a recording home to listen and study their responses to these phrases. A free interchange with another human being is the objective—an interchange of the hurts and weaknesses on the inside so the Lord may heal and repair earlier damage.

"Sandra, a crusty wall of fear around your spirit created during childhood has prevented you from fully maturing. Physically you are mature, but not inwardly. That wall of fear stunts the growth of certain characteristics. If we are emotionally hurt or put into great fear as a child, it begins to create a wall of fear (and hate in some cases) around your personality. The personality is not allowed to mature or grow as the body grows. The body goes on to advanced ages—ten, twenty, thirty, forty, and so on—but that phase of the child remains the same age, reliving the same emotional hurt. An example would be, in your case, the people making fun of your speech, your parents fighting, or reliving the same fear of your parents separating and you losing one or the other. It might be your fear of being left out and alone. That part of you has not grown up. There is still a portion of you that is that little child, a little child still hurt and fearful. Am I right?" I asked.

"Yes, I know you are right," Sandra replied with a sheepish grin on her face. "When I remember these things about myself, I often get tears in my eyes. I sometimes cry. People ask me why I'm crying. I tell them I don't know. I'd feel dumb saying I just thought about my childhood or something out of my childhood. Could it be the little child in me crying from the fears and hurts?" she asked as tears once again begin to well up in her eyes.

"Exactly," I replied. "Let me draw you another diagram. Let's make a circle and pretend that circle is the real you. Now, as you were hurt and subjected to fear as a child, a wall began to build up around the *real you*. You got so you would not trust people entirely. The wall began to exclude people from your life. In part, the little child in your past is now a loner. You don't show her to anyone for fear of criticism and further hurt. She is alone, unsubmitted.

Unexposed hurts weaknesses inside

"Sandra, do you find yourself speaking, understanding, and thinking as this hurt child inside of you? Does it appear that she sometimes controls your behavior?" I asked Sandra that question slowly, not wanting her to be afraid and not answer.

"Yes, I believe so," she answered. "Sometimes I don't act very mature. Even I can see that I am acting immature, so I know other people can see it," she said cautiously.

"That little child is in prison," I explained. "We are going to begin the process of freeing her. Paul in 1 Corinthians 13:11–13 says:

> *When I was a child, I spoke like a child, I thought like a child, I reasoned like a child; but when I became a man, I gave up childish ways. For now we see in a mirror dimly, but then face to face [we do not see or understand life because of this bound-up child]. Now I know in part; then I shall know fully, even as I have been fully known. So now faith, hope, and love abide, these three; but the greatest of these is love.*

Laying my Bible back on the corner of my desk I went on. "Through the love of Jesus, we can let Him go back and heal the love failure and fears of this child. This bound-up child will be set free by the love of our Lord. So you can *give up childish things*. Just like Jesus healed your heart from the broken relationships, He will heal the fears and hurts of this child. In 1 Corinthians 14:20, Paul says, 'Brothers, do not be children in your thinking. Be infants in evil, but in your thinking be mature.'" I stood, and taking the eraser, I began erasing the crusty wall of fear diagram and began writing in bold print. Sandra was beginning to write so she didn't miss anything.

"The healing power of Jesus will move you from A to B," I said. "He will set free the bondage of that little child." I moved back to my chair slowly. Large tears began to roll down Sandra's face.

She began to speak. "Jesus is healing that little child in my past right now, and we haven't even prayed yet. Oh, I love the Lord."

The presence of God began to fill the room. Joy permeated all of us. Her body and spirit glowed with excitement.

The Lord was healing that little child in bondage so Sandra could now understand as an adult and not as a child. She could now be freed of that fear and insecurity that was a carryover from childhood. "Thank you, Lord, for healing Sandra. Praise God! Praise God! Thank you, Lord."

Our voices were all in unity giving thanks to our Heavenly Father. Then it was quiet in the room. Tears were streaming down Sandra's face and onto her neck. She was not even aware of the tears as they dampened her clothing around her neck. The power of God was all over her. God was healing His child. Sandra had submitted to God and allowed Him to heal her. What a picture! James 5:16 says, "Therefore, confess your sins to one another and pray for one another, that you may be healed. The prayer of a righteous person has great power as it is working." Sandra had confessed to another, we had prayed, and God had healed. What a glorious sight!

It is so important to confess what is on the inside of the real you—the weaknesses, hurts, wrong goals, fears or guilt—so a submitted brother or sister can pray and God can heal. It is important at this juncture to notice that James is talking to brothers in James 5:12 who are in relationship spiritually to one another. Confession should only be to close, submitted believers in Jesus Christ. Confession to casual Christians usually causes trouble, not healing. People not in submitted relationships often use information from such confession for gossip and as a vehicle to belittle or criticize the person.

Confess and Forsake Wrong Behavior

"Whoever conceals his transgressions will not prosper, but he who confesses and forsakes them will obtain mercy" (Prov. 28:13). "Therefore, confess your sins to one another and pray for one another, that you may be healed. The prayer of a righteous person has great power as it is working" (James 5:16). Confession should be limited to one or two people you are in close relationship with, which would include a counselor with whom you can spend one or two hours building a trust relationship. A person who is suffering will receive healing and mercy if they follow these steps:

1. Submit to another submitted follower of Christ to help you.
2. Confess and admit faults.
3. Forsake and/or stop the wrong behavior.
4. Pray for one another.

Confession pushes out the guilt of the wrongful behavior.

A criminal act must be confessed by the person committing it. Some people are driven by guilt to police authorities so that confession can take place. The guilt leaves, but unless the other three steps are taken, the result is only short-lived, and the person is back in wrongful conduct. Build a relationship, confess the wrong, stop the act, and pray. That is the underlying procedure in counseling that will heal the injured spirit.

Confession of inner hurts, fears, and weaknesses in counseling sessions is not always possible or advisable for some people. Some things are best confessed only to a husband or wife, a pastor or a mentor—someone who is loyal and possesses sufficient compassion to love the person in trouble. You should become sensitive to entering into submitted relationships with the people God sends you. Never show conduct in attitude or speech that could be interpreted by the counselee as rejection of them as a person. But don't agree with the wrongful behavior either.

"Sandra, do you have a close girlfriend about your same age?" I asked.

"No," she responded with a puzzled look on her face.

"Is there some woman who seems to be interested in helping you that you may have ignored?"

"No, I don't believe so." Her voice trailed off. Then she spoke. "Wait. I do believe there is. Mary Baldwin has always shown a great deal of interest in me. Could it be that God sent her to be a close friend and sister to me? A submitted sister? She does seem so wise in matters pertaining to God.

Come to think about it, she is a well-balanced person. Maybe God did send her to me."

"Sandra, allow God to give birth to the submitted relationship. Do not push it. Just be open, and it will happen. You and your Christian friend can both draw strength from the relationship. Let me write a list of five rules in developing a submitted relationship." I stood by the chalkboard, and while I was talking, I erased the previous notes.

Rule One: Begin to Relax. I sat on the edge of the desk and explained. "Relax physically, mentally, and spiritually. Love cannot be received by a person who is uptight. Love cannot be received by a person who is struggling. Remember earlier when we talked about the struggling, non-swimmer child? There is a peace, and there is a rest for God's people. But as Hebrews 4 says, we cannot enter this rest until we cease from our own works. We must reestablish our goals. Stop taking excess thought of (a) food, drink, clothes, or shelter, (b) making ourselves a big deal, and (c) tomorrow or the future. Jesus said to take no thought of these things. Matthew 6:33 says, 'But seek first the kingdom of God and His righteousness [right relationships with God and people], and all these things will be added to you.'

"Stop the struggle. Relax and enter into the rest, and then you can begin to open up in building submitted relationships. You will not be meeting people just to foster and promote yourself. It is only when you reestablish your goals (cease from your own works) that you will be able to develop a person-to-person relationship that is open—a relationship where the truth can be spoken in love without fear of wrong motives or selfish gain. True loyalty can be developed. When loyalty is present in a relationship, peace and trust follow." I moved back to the board and wrote.

Rule Two: Be Sensitive to Who God Sends You. "The second step to enter a submitted relationship is to be sensitive to who God sends to you. You can only have submitted relationships with one to possibly seven people. For most of us, five significant relationships will be more than enough to occupy our time—a husband, a wife, a child, a pastor, a sibling, a coworker, and so on. These will be people who will have loyalty that you can discern in their spirit, a relationship that withstands an all-night illness. It's a responsible attitude to the relationship where your sister sits all day with you or you with her if the circumstances demand. Become sensitive to who God has sent to you. And become sensitive that God also sends you to other people. But remember, you may be acquainted with dozens of people and see them frequently, but only intimately are you related to a few."

Rule Three: Accept People as They Are. This time I moved back to my chair, leaned forward, and began to explain the last step I had written on the board. "To enter into a submitted relationship is to accept people as they are. Don't try to change them. Accept yourself as you are, and accept others as they are. Your motivation as you enter into the submitted relationship is to love and help that person—not change them. Don't try to control, manipulate, or reform them.

Accept them as they are so you can both begin to start being honest with one another. Schedule a weekly lunch or coffee. Schedule a time you can regularly see one another to develop a trusted relationship. No gossip. Just a real building of a relationship on a one-on-one basis. You will find that you'll start telling her your fears. You will find yourself sharing early life experiences. Some of these experiences will expose hurts and injuries you need to deal with as we have done in this session.

"You have shared a few of those hurts with me. However, you'll find that as you enter a God-inspired and submitted relationship, you'll expose and receive healing for even more hurts, fears, and weaknesses that still may remain. This counseling session has only been a Band-Aid program to get you by until you can enter into closer, deeper, relationships with Richard and another one or two people. It may be that God will send a husband and wife to you and Richard to relate to. Whatever happens, just be sensitive to who it is, and do not act hastily. To be sensitive means to be gentle and slow. God will confirm in several ways to whom you are to relate. As you move into relationships with the person, be willing to accept their success and failure.

"Sandra! Don't look at me so strange! Everyone has failures. As you share your fears, weaknesses, and hurts, what do you think they will be doing? It is a mutual relationship for the good of all people involved. They will also look to you for guidance and love. Be open to share and comfort. Like any new relationship, there is always a honeymoon period. When you and Richard were newly married, did you not have a few months of little or no problems and just exciting joy?"

Sandra looked toward Cloetta, hesitated for a moment, and then sheepishly replied, "Yes and I would give anything to recapture that period of time. What went wrong? We have just kind of drifted apart."

"The answer to that question, Sandra, lies in the fact that God united Sandra and Richard together so you would each have someone to look to for comfort. You each have needs that are to be met. You both have fears, weaknesses, and hurts that need to be dealt with. In part, God sent you to each other for that reason—to meet the needs and help heal the hurts. After the honeymoon period is over, the relationship will die unless you both begin opening up and moving into a deeper commitment toward one another. Many people, not understanding the purposes of a relationship, fail to use this opportunity to heal and also heal the hurts of their previous life.

"The Lord says in Ephesians 5, that even before a wife is to submit and a husband is to love, both *submit themselves to one another in the fear of God.* Opening ourselves up to one another is a condition precedent to a wife submitting and a husband loving. It must be done first. Submitting to one another is done in the honeymoon period. Opening up to one another is begun during the honeymoon period and is a continual process. As husband and wife open up and reveal inner secrets of the hurts, the fears, and the weaknesses, the Lord backs them up. You shouldn't try to change one another. You should try to change yourself. You must submit (conform) to one another, and the Lord will back you up." Each time I moved toward the chalkboard to write, Sandra picked up the pencil so she, too, would be ready to write.

Rule Four: Give Up Personal Desires for the Good of the Relationship. I slid back into my chair and looked toward Cloetta and then back at Sandra. "Step number four in building a submitted relationship is giving up personal desire for the good of the relationship. "When I first married Cloetta, she liked to ride bicycles and take walks. I thought bicycles and walking around the block with my wife was kid-stuff, not something a *man* should be seen doing. I discovered after several months of marriage that I needed to give up some of my personal desires for the good of the relationship. Had I not done this, the relationship would not have grown."

Sandra looked toward Cloetta and smiled. Cloetta returned her smile quickly and spoke. "I gave up some of my personal desires also."

I smiled. "We all have a deep inner longing for closeness to another human being. If the moment of truth in which to open up comes in a relationship and I balk and refuse to open up, I will turn away. I will seek a satisfaction for this inner emptiness elsewhere—perhaps in my work, perhaps in my play such as golf, football, or tennis—supplying a substitute for my need of close friends. If you have balked at opening up, I encourage you to turn back again to the God-given relationship and begin anew. If you don't, these fears, hurts, and weaknesses will remain with you for life. The Lord has provided this medicine of interrelationship with one another. Use it. Explore it. Receive the healing. Give up personal desires for the good of the relationship, and submit to one another.

Chapter 12

Fruits of the Spirit

"Mr. Religion" frequently speaks out and declares, "Oh, brother Keene, I walk in the Spirit." It sounds good, but before a man can walk in the Spirit, he must learn to live *in* the Spirit. I believe the next time I'm asked to help select a new pastor for a church from the ninety-three applicants that were called by God while they were walking in the Spirit, I will notify them that we will be sending deacons to live in their homes for a week. That way we can see if the prospective man of faith and power has really got it together with his sheep at home. I suspect once we notify them of this procedure, ninety-two of the applicants will tell us that God is calling them elsewhere.

The first three fruits listed in Galatians 5 deal with the self-to-self relationship (love, joy, peace). Here is where we learn to live with ourselves—no inner conflict. As one begins to establish these fruits in his life, he begins to live in the Spirit. The next three fruits deal with the self-to-others relationship (patience, kindness, goodness). These are truly fruits of the Spirit that affect other people. These fruits of the Holy Spirit are for the benefit of others. The last three fruits deal with the self-to-God relationship (faithfulness, gentleness, self-control). Now a man is walking in the Spirit. If we live in the Spirit, let us also walk in the Spirit. Let us not desire vain glory, provoking one another, envying one another.

"By the way, Sandra, I now enjoy walking around the neighborhood and riding bicycles. After sixteen years of marriage I even enjoy helping Cloetta do dishes, cook, and make beds. Note one thing: I do not need to do these things often but just be willing to give up my desire to watch television or play golf for the good of my husband-wife relationship."

Sandra stood and spoke. "Could I bring Richard down here for you to talk to him? I want him to have that kind of attitude!"

"Yes, Sandra, I'll talk to Richard. But remember to be the attitude leader or pacesetter. As you set this attitude of giving up personal desires for the good of the relationship, Richard will follow. Men generally follow whatever attitude their wife sets. If she is bitter and grouchy, so follows the husband. If she is pleasant and sensitive to her husband, he will tend to follow."

Rule Number Five: Entering into Relationships Is to Receive Inner Healing as We Have Done in This Counseling Session. "Before we conclude this session, I want to give you the last step in healing the hurts in your spirit that have been caused by father, mother, teacher, brother, boyfriend, husband, preacher, friend, and so on.

"Let's read Mark 11:22–26." Cloetta handed Sandra a Bible opened to Mark. As soon as Sandra found the verse, she looked up, and I began to read.

> *And Jesus answered them, "Have faith in God. Truly, I say to you, whoever says to this mountain, 'Be taken up and thrown into the sea,' and does not doubt in his heart, but believes that what he says will come to pass, it will be done for him. Therefore I tell you, whatever you ask in prayer, believe that you have received it, and it will be yours. And whenever you stand praying, forgive, if you have anything against anyone, so that*

> *your Father also who is in heaven may forgive you your trespasses."*

"The point that this step makes is that the answer to your prayers is directly related to your forgiving those people who have wronged you. Your prayers are empty if you do not, as an act of your will, forgive these people. These old hurts with the accompanying bitterness and unforgiveness often prevent the Lord from answering the prayers. First John 3:22–23 also confirms that God will answer our prayers, but we must keep His commandments by believing in Jesus and loving one another. We cannot love one another if we hold bitterness within us. Confess it to a submitted brother, have them pray, and be healed (James 5:16)."

I looked down at my watch. It was now 5:05 p.m. We had spent three hours counseling. "Sandra, is there anything that comes to mind that you would like to discuss before we finish?" I asked.

"All I can say is whoo! I have never been so bandaged with truth in my life. I am excited. I feel like a new person. I'm anxious to begin doing the things you've told me. But how can I remember all this? Won't I forget?" she asked.

I looked toward Cloetta, and she reached out, handing me a book. "Take this book and read it. Share it with others. If you have questions, please feel free to call us at any time."

Sandra read the cover: *Please Don't Hurt Me.*

"Now the last step to heal the hurt is to remember to

pray for the person who hurt you," I told her. "Shall we join hands and pray?"

Five Steps to Counseling

The discussion with Sandra is now the fifth step in the five steps to counseling. For review I have listed the five steps below.

1. Build the relationship
    a. By exhorting
    b. By encouraging
    c. By charging
2. Confess the fault
3. Forsake the fault
4. Pray
5. Encourage entry into submitted relationships

Epilogue

Two days later on a Friday evening, I received a telephone call from Richard, Sandra's husband. His first comment was this: "What did you do to my wife?"

With some caution I replied, "What do you mean?"

"She's a new person. I've never seen anything like it. I've got a brand-new wife. It's terrific. What did you do? I must know. Can I come and talk with you?"

I set up a time for Richard to stop by. What Richard was experiencing was the joy that comes from a wife who truly is submitting to his plans and his love. He could detect that Sandra was now receiving his love. This made him want to love her more. Sandra was now fitting into his plans. If Richard decided to move to Alaska, Sandra would go without a hassle.

When Richard stopped by to see me, he brought Sandra. What a joy to see two happy people on their second honeymoon. They were both beaming with excitement. Sandra commented, “Mr. Keene, I’ve never been so happy in all my life. Thank you. Oh, thank you.”

My reply was simple. “Don’t thank me, Sandra. Thank God for His healing power. God heals the hurts and takes the pain away. We are serving a great Heavenly Father.”

About the Author

Davis Keene is a follower of Jesus, husband and leader who cares deeply about faith, family, and the long-term impact of the choices we make. His work is shaped by the teachings of his grandfather, the original teacher behind Please Don't Hurt Me, and whose wisdom around relationships and responsibility played a formative role in his life. Davis writes from the lived experience of himself and generations before him, not theory. He understands the tension between success and presence, ambition and relationship, and the challenge of building a healthy family in a fast-paced world. His focus is on helping people think clearly about how they treat one another and how those patterns shape families over time. His hope is to help others build lives and families marked by intention, care, and lasting influence.

www.ingramcontent.com/pod-product-compliance
Lightning Source LLC
LaVergne TN
LVHW020632100826
845148LV00012B/2160